Seeing "Flower Petals" Reveal Themselves Slowly:

A Guide To Understanding and Interpreting The Parables of Jesus

James F. Malerba

BookLocker

Saint Petersburg, Florida

Print ISBN: 978-1-64718-872-6
Epub ISBN: 978-1-64718-873-3
Mobi ISBN: 978-1-64718-874-0

Published by BookLocker.com, Inc., St. Petersburg, Florida.

Printed on acid-free paper.

BookLocker.com, Inc.
2020

First Edition

Library of Congress Cataloging in Publication Data
Malerba, James F.
Seeing "Flower Petals" Reveal Themselves Slowly: A Guide To Understanding and Interpreting The Parables of Jesus by James F. Malerba
Library of Congress Control Number: 2020916384

Dedication

It is with great love and pride that I dedicate this book to my children, Jennifer and James, my daughter-in-law Lori, and my four grandchildren, Hannah, Alexa, David and James, who have been such a great source of joy and happiness in my life, and who make every day a wonderful and blessed experience. They mean everything to me and are the light of my life.

To Joanne:

Thank you for being such a kind and lovely person. It is with pleasure I send this book, and I hope you enjoy it.

Best Wishes,
Jim

About the Author

James F. Malerba is a writer and editor who worked in the corporate and healthcare industries for more than 35 years. He also published dozens of feature articles in newspapers and magazines across the country on a variety of topics ranging from healthcare and political issues to interviews with noted Catholics. He is a graduate of the Yale University Divinity School with a master's degree in Religion and a concentration in New Testament Studies. Earlier this year, he published a book entitled, "God is Everywhere – Even in Nursery Rhymes!" That work not only presents beloved and timeless rhymes, but also has commentaries showing how God is in each one. Thus, both children and adults can benefit from its contents. Malerba lives in the New Haven, Connecticut area.

Table of Contents

Section I – Introduction and Background

Over the past 100 years or so, theologians and New Testament scholars have devoted themselves to the various meanings contained in the parables of Jesus. Almost unanimously, they agree that the parables describe the kingdom of God and prepare people to enter heaven through good works during their lives on Earth.

One such expert, C.H. Dodd, saw end-times messages, or eschatology, as the central message in the parables. In fact, many in the early Church were convinced that the *Parousia*, or end of the world, would occur in their lifetime. Obviously, that did not happen. Dodd suggested that Jesus preached a *realized* eschatology; in other words, fulfilling the word of God through the Son. (https://en.wikipedia.org/wiki/C._H._Dodd)

As we will soon see, the eschatological, or matters of end times, message in some parables, such as the wicked tenants, the unprepared wedding guest, Lazarus and the rich man, and others, comes through all too clearly: To those who believe, eternal life beckons. To those who do not believe or lead lives of unrepentant sin, no salvation comes to them. Yet, as in all parables, there are underlying, subtle messages for us to unpeel that shed even greater light and understanding on those immortal sayings of the Lord in the gospels.

That view was underscored by Leander Keck, professor emeritus of New Testament Studies at the Yale Divinity School. Like C.H. Dodd, Keck saw the parables as extended metaphors. He said this about interpreting them: "Jesus introduced a strange way of being in the world, a way that could be grasped only through the indirection of stories of familiar life which were both and were not 'the kingdom.'"*

*From Professor Keck's lecture on September 25, 1991.

1

Though reward and punishment permeate many of Jesus' parables, others contain messages containing hope or instructional messages that serve to enlighten one and all. Each has a richness peculiar to itself that must be uncovered through reasoned study and interpretation. All parables in the synoptic gospels present this challenge to the curious reader. A casual reading produces a basic understanding of the meaning of a given parable but does not delve too deeply into the wonderful "hidden" messages it contains.

Just as flowers "awaken" by opening their petals slowly when spring arrives, so it is when we enhance our understanding of the timeless messages in the parables of Jesus. We do not experience a thunderbolt of sudden enlightenment; rather, we open the petals of our minds slowly, and greater understanding comes in good time.

Becoming enlightened, then, is a process. Jesus Himself noted this when he said, "Is a lamp brought in to be placed under a bushel basket or under a bed, and not placed on a lampstand? For there is nothing hidden except to be made visible; nothing is secret except to come to light" (Mark 4:21-22). That was a message not only for the disciples, but also for all people, then and today. We who have been given the wonderful gift of faith must not keep it to ourselves but are to spread it to all through our Christian love and words and deeds.

Characteristics of the Parables

In the late 19th and early 20the centuries, a technique that became known as form criticism became a popular method for biblical scholars to look at books of the Bible, including the gospels, and interpret the structure of their messages. The biggest proponent of form criticism was Rudolph Bultmann, a German biblical scholar, who used this method to note theme and literary patterns in the parables and other sayings of Jesus. According to Bultmann, the following are common characteristics of every parable of Jesus:

1. Only necessary persons appear. For example, in the Prodigal Son, there is a father but no mother. Seldom are there more than two persons, and in any parable with more than two people, only two speakers are present at the same time.

2. There is never parallel action, just a consecutive sequence.

3. Characters all possess one trait – the judge is unjust, five virgins are wise and five foolish, Lazarus is poor and the homeowner rich, and so forth.

4. Parables are usually devoid of emotion, unless Jesus is making a point requiring it. Examples are the unmerciful servant and the Good Samaritan.

5. Some parables leave the reader guessing. The rich fool, the prudent servant, and the barren fig tree's fates are not revealed.

6. Also, a detail or two might be missing. We are never told how the steward wasted his master's goods, just that he did it.

7. In most parables the most important item comes at the end. The sower, the talents, and the Pharisee and the publican are such examples.

8. Jesus invited the judgment of the listener, though he never judged the characters in his own parables. However, some judgment is at least implied – Pharisee and the tax collector, two sons, and the Prodigal Son.

    (from Boltmann, Rudolph, *History of the Synoptic Tradition*, 1921)

A striking similarity of the forms of Jesus' parables can be found in Aesop's Fables, which also preached messages of reward and punishment, the necessity for leading a good life, and other aphorisms intended to raise the intellectual thought of his audiences. Here is an example:

"A farmer caught a fox that was destroying his vines and garden. To kill the fox, the farmer set fire to the fox's tail and turned it loose. In torment, the fox ran straight into the farmer's grain fields, setting fire to the crop, which was especially abundant that year. Though the farmer ran after the fox, he was too late. His crop was totally destroyed."

That fable, as with all of Aesop's fables, contains only one central message. In this case, the desire for revenge on the fox stands out. While Aesop did not intend to convey a spiritual message, the lesson he intended suffices: revenge does not always work, and the "reward" of killing the fox came at a very high cost to the agonized farmer.

In a way, that fable resonates in the parable of the rich fool (Luke 12:16-21), where the rich man wants to tear down his barns and build larger ones, thus enjoying unlimited wealth and prosperity. Unfortunately for him, God had bad news – his life ended that very night he set up his ambitious plans. So, too, the farmer in the fable came to a bad end, at least in terms of going broke that year, while the rich fool did not account for the fact he would be called by God to answer for his life's works.

Why Did Jesus Employ Parables?

As stated in Matthew (13:10-15), the disciples asked Jesus why he was speaking to the people, including the Jewish religious leaders of the time, in parables. Jesus answered that while the disciples had been granted understanding of the kingdom of heaven, others "look but do not see and hear but do not understand."

Thus, Jesus was fulfilling the prophecy of Isaiah (6:9-10), who said, "Gross is the heart of this people, they will hardly hear with their ears, they have closed their eyes, lest they see with their eyes and hear with their ears..." So, Jesus left it to his hearers to interpret his words, interpreting parables only to his own disciples and no one else. He did promise, though, that those who heard, listened, and had a change of heart would understand (Matthew. 13:12).

Rabbinic Parables Preceded Jesus

While all Christians are familiar with the Lord's parables, there were Rabbinic parables that preceded Jesus. Some were themes Jesus used when relating parables to his various audiences. of his parables. Also, the rabbinic parables often opened with words similar to those the Lord used: "The kingdom of heaven is like (may be likened)" (Matthew 13:24). So, when Jesus drew on the similar words spoken by earlier rabbis, he was imparting to his listeners both themes and language with which they would have been familiar. Our next example uses an identical opening.

Witness this one, attributed to <u>Babylonian Talmud</u>, *Shabbat^h* 153a

Then Solomon in his wisdom said: "Let your garments always be white, and let not your head lack oil (Ecclesiastes 9:8).

Rabbi Johanan ben Zakkai said:

"To what is this matter likened? This is like a king who summoned his servants to a banquet, but he did not set a time for them. The attentive got themselves dressed and sat at the door of the king's house. They said: 'Is anything missing at the king's house?' The foolish went on with their work. They said: 'Is there any banquet without toil?'

"Suddenly, the king summoned his servants. The attentive gathered before him, all dressed up., while the foolish gathered before him all soiled. The king was pleased with the attentive, but angry with the foolish. He said: 'Let those who are dressed up for the banquet sit, eat and drink; but let those who did not dress for this banquet stand and watch.'"

That parable is, in its theme, quite similar to the one Jesus told of the wedding banquet, in which one guest arrived without wearing proper wedding attire. Most guests arrived dressed for a wedding, one did not. He was bound and thrown out of the banquet hall (Matthew 22:1-10).

There is a similar ending in the Rabbinic parable, except those who did not arrive dressed properly were forced to stand and watch the others eat, drink and celebrate. In a way, their punishment was just as great as the man in the wedding parable of Jesus, because they could only long for the good food and drink to which the other guests were privy.

Rabbi Simeon ben Johai said:

"From this we know Israel will not face Gehinnom forever." He proposed a parable:

"To what is this matter likened? To a king of flesh and blood who had a swampy field. Some men came and leased it for ten khors (= 60 bushels) of wheat a year. They fertilized it, watered it and harvested it. But they gathered no more than one khor of wheat during the year. The king said to them: What is this?' They said to him: 'You know, our Lord (and) king, at first you gathered nothing from the field you gave us. And now we have fertilized and watered it and have gathered at least one khor of wheat.' So Israel shall plead before the Holy One, blessed be He!: Lord, you know the evil impulse incites us!"

Parables and Fables – the Differences

As we have seen, the rabbinic parables and Aesop's Fables all have moral lessons for the reader. They are cautionary tales to urge people to follow the straight and narrow. Jesus' parables also conveyed moral messages, but with heavenly or spiritual consequences or rewards.

In the same way, the parables of Jesus involved "real" people to whom all listeners could relate – the rich man and Lazarus, the Prodigal Son, and others. In fables (Aesop's and others), the people and events were pure fiction, though certainly memorable and entertaining.

We are all interpreters

We all interpret things we see or hear. Sometimes we might be spot on; other times, we might be far off. The beauty of our interpretive ability lies not in what might be right or wrong, but rather in how we see things.

Take a sporting event, for example. You and a friend go to a baseball game and see exactly the same thing. On the way home, you both compare verbal notes regarding things that happened during the game. You thought the pitcher really had is good "stuff" that day. Your friend might have a different opinion, saying he thought the pitcher looked tired and not on his game, though he won.

Similarly, look at a piece of art more than once. It is almost a certainty that when you see the same painting again you will find things you did not notice the first time. It could be the color scheme, the expression on a face, or just about anything else. The fact is that you can almost always come up with a different interpretation the second time and beyond. That is the joy of interpreting.

So, in the parables, the following might be useful in getting more out of each parable, enriching your spiritual experience.

1. Note the setting of the parable. What text precedes and follows it? To whom was Jesus addressing the parable, and why?

2. Pay attention to the wording, "plot," and suspense, if any. Always keep in mind that parables are studies, as well as lessons. Also, where applicable, compare, where applicable, alike parables across the synoptic gospels, noting all the similarities and differences among them.

3. Be sure to read every parable in its historical context, always keeping form-critical methods in mind. In other words, don't put a modern "spin" on them, except to say how the message in a given parable would apply in today's world. Focus instead on the gospel writer's intent and his early Christian audience.

4. Who are the main "characters" in the parable, and what are their similarities and differences? Often, these characters provide clues related to the main point Jesus was making.

5. It also is important to understand there were two sets of audiences for all the parables – the original audiences addressed by Jesus, and members of the early Church to whom the evangelists were writing.

6. Do not over-interpret a parable, which is easy enough to do. Rather, note carefully what happens at the end of a parable as a clue to ascertaining its meaning. This is called the "rule of end stress" by New Testament scholars.

7. Place the message of a given parable in the context of Jesus' earthly ministry. You will discover that most of the parables deal with the kingdom of God – either its inauguration or consummation – and discipleship within the present phase of the kingdom in expectation of the consummation.

The Enigma of Q

Before addressing the parables themselves, let us examine the so-called "Q" source. Q is an abbreviation for the German word "Quelle," which means *source*. Many modern-day New Testament scholars have spent years dissecting the parables in Matthew and Luke and ultimately concluding they contain a number of them that both gospel writers took from a source that, alas, no longer exists – if it ever did. (The Q source is not found in Mark's gospel.) In effect, then, Q is a source that does not appear to exist. It is kind of like trying to describe black holes in deep space. You can't see them because they absorb even light, but astronomers know they exist.

Q first came to light in 1838 when a German scholar named Christian Hermann Weisse offered a theory that beneath certain parables – most notably those in Matthew and Luke – there was evidence of another, unknown source. Then, in 1945, two brothers in Egypt dug up an earthen jar, which contained 12 books bound in leather. Experts named these volumes the Nag Hammadi Library. They contained a complete copy of the gospel of Thomas, written in Coptic. After translating the gospel into Greek, scholars made valid comparisons between sayings in the gospel of Thomas and with the sayings in the synoptic gospels.

Interest in Q continued, and in 1989, James Robinson of the Institute for Antiquity and Christianity in Claremont, California, began a task that was to take 10 years to complete. Robinson and his staff took the parables verse by verse and word by word and ultimately published an enormous volume called "The Critical Edition of Q."

So, scholars look for similarities in Matthew's and Luke's gospels to substantiate the existence of Q. In many cases, both writers used wording that was almost identical. For example, Matthew 6:24 is the same as Luke 6:13. Also, Matthew 7:7-8 and Luke 11: 9-10 are very similar. It is perhaps no coincidence that those two gospel writers recorded the Sermon on the Mount in the same order.

Here are the Q parables found only in Matthew and Luke:

Burglar – Matthew 24:43; Luke 12:39

Servant put in charge – Matthew 24:45; Luke 12:42

Leaven – Matthew 13:33; Luke 13:20

Great supper – Matthew 22:1; Luke 14:16

Lost sheep – Matthew 18:12; Luke 15:3

Talents – Matthew 25:14; Luke 19:12

In addition to the parables common to Matthew and Luke, there is other material peculiar to those two gospel writers, from the preaching of John the Baptist to the many lessons Jesus taught his audiences, such as treasure in heaven, divisions in families, and settling out of court.

We can only trust the scholars' in-depth research, much of which is remarkably similar, especially in their conclusions, regarding the existence of the Q source. The following address this topic in detail:

Arthur Bellinzoni, Jr., Joseph Tyson, & William Walker, editors, "The Existence of Q", at:
http://earlychristianwritings.com/q-exist.html

Marliyn Mellows, "More about Q and the Gospel of Thomas," at:
www.pbs.org/wgbh/pages/frontline/shows/religion/story/qthomas.html

James Robinson, "The Real Jesus of the Sayings 'Q' Gospel," at:
www.religion-online.org/showarticle.sep?title=542

As you have seen, the Q source would appear to have had a profound influence on Mathew and Luke. Unfortunately, we will never have a definitive answer; the enigma remains.

That said, we now move along to the "main event" – our interpretation of those wonderful parables the Lord spoke for his audience and for us all. Please enjoy this journey as you enhance your understanding of the wonderful gems given to us by the Son of God.

Section II – Parables of Seeds and the Land

The Sower of Seeds of Faith (Matthew 13:3-9; Mark 4:3-9; Luke 8:5-8)

The theme of the sower parable is simple enough. A farmer planted seeds and looked forward to enjoying the bounty of his crop. He was a specialist, just as today's workers all have their own specialty. So, he had to be very meticulous, to ensure he would get maximum results from the field where the seeds were being planted. As the parable tells us, that was not fully the case.

Jesus carefully mentioned that some seed fell on the path next to the field. The birds flew in and ate up this seed, so there could be no growth resulting from that wasted effort. Some seeds fell on rocky ground, which had a dearth of soil, so again there could be no crop growing. Even worse, some seed fell among thorns, which choked the plants that arose. Finally, some seed fell on rich soil and yielded an abundant crop.

So, was the sower sloppy in his work? Should he not have been more careful as to where the seeds went? Not at all! In ancient Israel, there were no automated methods for spreading seeds. It was tedious work in the hot sun and the sower was at the mercy of the prevailing wind, as well. Little wonder, then, that some seed went to waste, though at least those which fell on the path helped nourish the birds. Such was not what happened to the seeds that fell among thorns. But the message in the parable is that not all seed went to waste. Far from it. That which fell on fertile soil flourished.

The sower was, of course, Jesus himself and – without specifically saying it – he was underscoring the free will God gave to all humans. Some who hear Jesus' words (then and now) are represented by the seed

17

that fell on the path. They have no root in faith and Satan (the bird) snatches them up to himself. Seeds that end up on rocky soil represent those who hear the word of God but are joyous only briefly, falling back to their old ways because they have no roots to anchor their faith. Similarly, the seed among thorns bears no fruit because those people are consumed with earthly concerns, especially riches.

Conversely, the seed falling on rich soil reaps untold rewards. Those who are truly enlightened and eager to embrace the gospel bear "fruit" up to one hundredfold, not only embracing God but also sharing their faith with others, thus increasing their reward exponentially.

Did Jesus' words have a positive effect on those who heard the parable? Perhaps yes, but more likely his many listeners were confused as to what Jesus was trying to tell them. The disciples certainly did not understand the message, because they asked him to explain it to them. Jesus did so, and when the disciples asked why he spoke in parables, the Lord said to the Twelve, "Because knowledge of the mysteries of the kingdom of heaven have been granted to you, but to them it has not been granted" (Matthew. 13:11).

That rather abrupt statement might lead the reader to believe that Jesus was deliberately excluding people from the Faith. But there is a deeper reason in that statement. Being the Son of God, Jesus knew that many of those hearing his words would neither heed them nor follow his way. The parable, therefore, as with his others, was intended to convey a lesson, as well as a caution. The disciples did not understand the sower parable to its extent, raising the question as to why Jesus spoke in parables at all. This showed an intellectual hunger and an eagerness to learn more about what the Lord was preaching.

Jesus was not the first to tell his audience that they had a lack of understanding. The prophet Isaiah, more than six hundred years earlier, said much the same thing:

"You shall indeed but not understand, you shall indeed look but never see. Gross is the heart of this people, they will hardly hear with their ears, they have closed their eyes, lest they see with their eyes and hear with their ears and understand with their heart and be converted, and I heal them" (Isaiah 6:9-10).

In today's world, untold millions of people reflect Isaiah's words, closing their ears and eyes and turning to the temptations the world offers everyone. Those who have either given up their faith (the seeds falling on rocky soil) or have never known God (the seeds on the path) are the ones whom Jesus had in mind. We see that attendance at religious services in virtually every faith tradition has fallen to all-time lows. Those who still are observant and practice their faith regularly, however, are the ones who bear fruit that yields "a hundred, sixty or thirtyfold" (Matthew. 13:23).

God does not force people to love him; rather, he created the human race with free will as part of our makeup. We can accept God, reject him, or ignore him. The parable of the sower is not just a lesson, but also a cautionary account for one and all. The richer the soil on which people sprout, the stronger they are in faith and devotion. "Blessed are the clean of heart, for they will see God" (Matthew 5:8).

Satan in the Growing Wheat (Matthew 13:24-30)

This parable is found only in Matthew. Though similar to the parable of the sower in that it also involves wheat, there is a major difference. We encounter a landowner, his (unknown and unseen) enemy, and the landowner's slaves.

Just as the sower had good luck with much of the sown crop, so did the landowner (or householder) who also was the sower. Here, however, there is a devious twist. Satan (the enemy) did his best to turn people away from the faith by sowing his seeds of sin among the believers. The weed in this parable was darnel, a destructive weed that, when first growing, resembles wheat.

The slaves, who could be said to represent the apostles, approached the householder, puzzled as to why weeds grew up with the valuable wheat crop. Should they just remove the weeds (unfaithful people) from the crop? No, said Jesus (the householder). That would be wrong, since you will probably destroy the good with the bad. Jesus used this parable to send a strong message to His disciples. The good would always be rewarded, the bad always punished.

The weeds (those who reject God) have every opportunity to repent and come into the faith and be one with the Creator. Jesus patiently explained this to his disciples, noting he was the sower of good seed (all people in the world) in the field (the world itself), and giving them the chance to embrace and grow in communion with God.

The weeds (Satan and his angels) descend upon God's children and try to lure them away from leading a clean life, free from serious sin. The harvest is thus the day of reckoning for the entire world, when Jesus will judge the living and the dead. The harvesters are the angels of God, who will collect the faithful for heaven. In one his most pointed warnings to those who are guilty of sin, Jesus said:

"The Son of Man will send his angels, and they will collect out of his kingdom all who cause others to sin and all evildoers. They will throw them into the fiery furnace [hell], where there will be wailing and grinding of teeth. Then the righteous will shine like the sun in the kingdom of their Father." (Matthew 13:41-43).

Harsh words from the Lord, but there is also a subtle message in his statement. We have a lifelong opportunity to believe in God or not, and to be given many opportunities to be faithful or to cave in to the devil. In other words, there is always hope – until death – that those who do not believe are the weeds who will not see God but rather will be punished for all eternity. The wheat – all believers – will be gathered up and saved in the "barn" of heaven, also for all eternity, reaping the reward of their faith on Earth. Where there is life, there is hope.

Section III – Satisfying Hunger with Faith

Enough Bread for a Crowd (Matthew 13:33)

As if to emphatically underscore his message of good and evil, Jesus veered a bit and gave the disciples additional food for thought – literally. The parable of the yeast showed us the Lord's subtle way of introducing the disciples to the all-important role they were to play following the Resurrection.

The brief parable of the woman preparing to make loaves of bread seems simple enough on the surface. As Jesus noted, she put three measures of wheat into wheat flour and waited until the yeast had leavened the dough. Why did Jesus specifically emphasize three measures of yeast?

That might sound like a small amount, but in reality – and the disciples would have been able to relate to this – the woman could have been able to make enough bread to feed about one hundred people with those three measures. Never mind that she would not have had a big enough oven, she could not have contained that much rising dough in her kitchen!

Jesus was foretelling his disciples that they (the measures of wheat) were to spread the gospel and expand the Faith (the dough) to one and all. The "bread" they would leaven was the Eucharist, the greatest spiritual gift in all of human history. Thus, the disciples were to spread out into the world and bring the message and Real Presence of Christ to full fruition, which would be revealed to them at the Last Supper.

Note: This parable used leaven as a positive force. It is the only statement of leavening as a good thing. Otherwise, Jesus and others cautioned against the leaven of the Pharisees and Sadducees, who "leavened" their teachings in a corrupt manner. (See Matthew, 16:5-12, Mark 8:15-21, Luke 12:1, 1 Corinthians 5:6-8, and Galatians, 5:9).

How Does Your Seed Grow? (Mark 4:26-29)

Many of us grow vegetable or flower gardens, and we often check them to see how the growth is coming. Honestly, though, do we really wonder how the seed grows by itself into a plant or flower?

Referring to the kingdom of God, Jesus told the disciples (following his explanation of the parable of the sower) that a sower of seeds finished the task and rested in sleep. Yet, this man did not really rest; rather, he checked night and day to see if the seeds were about to produce wheat.

As usual, Jesus was speaking to the disciples in parables, using metaphors of land, seed and growth. The sower merely started the process; nature did the rest. First, the seed sprouted the blade, then the ear, and finally the full grain in the ear. At that point, the landowner came out to reap the harvest, the reward for his initial work of sowing the seed earlier.

Let's interpret this parable. The sower was Jesus, who, through the disciples, sowed the seeds of faith. Those who then hear the words of salvation and heed them were the men and women accepting the way to eternal life. So, the fully grown wheat plant represented the person of faith, and the harvester (God) gathers the harvest into Himself.

A vivid example of this is found in 1 Timothy (2:5-7), where Saint Paul states unequivocally that "For this I was appointed preacher and apostle...teacher of the Gentiles in faith and truth." This is an ongoing Pauline theme, reminding those to whom his letters are addressed that the seeds of faith are absolutely indispensable if we are to grow in Christ.

The Mustard Seed – but no Jar (Matthew 13:31-32; Mark 4:31-32)

In a brief and simple parable also hinting at spiritual growth, Jesus said the mustard seed is insignificant in size, but mighty in growth. There are a couple of ways to look at this parable. First, the tiny mustard seed can refer to our baptism, conferred when most of us were little infants. As we began to grow and learned about God, that little seed began to sprout growth, which continued into adulthood. The birds (our children) later nested in our teaching about faith in God and began their own journey to deeper understanding of how we must live to someday enter eternal life.

Also, that same seed we are given charges us with spreading the faith through our good words and deeds as Christians. Those large branches mentioned by Jesus are all of us who are eager to not only to live exemplary lives, but also to be role models for or children, grandchildren, friends, and all others whose lives we touch. The Lord emphasized this in John's gospel (15:1-17) in his final discourse to the disciples: "I am the vine, you are the branches. Whoever remains in me and I in him, will bear much fruit..." (John 15:5). That was the charge set down to be followed forever. We cannot bear fruit without faith in Jesus.

Section IV – Serendipity over Found Treasures

An Ancient Lottery (Sort of) Winner (Matthew: 13:44)

Two of the shortest parables of Jesus also are those of great meaning – the buried treasure and the pearl of great price. We will examine the treasure parable first.

A man digs in a field and finds a treasure busied in the ground. He buries it again, and then buys the field in which the treasure lies. The treasure, of course, is a found faith, which then ultimately leads to eternal happiness. But there is more than meets the eye.

Because of the Roman occupation, and taxes on the Jewish citizens, it was not uncommon for someone with a good deal of money or other assets to bury them in a field. That way, the ancient form of tax evasion saved a person's money for his own use later. This is where questions might well occur regarding the new buyer's actions.

First, he did not own the field but had to purchase it, which he did. Second, was the man who bought the field stealing someone else's hard-earned money? Third, did he perhaps know that the former owner of the field – if he, indeed, was also the one who buried the treasure – had passed away or moved somewhere else without digging up his booty?

The answer is – none of the above. Jesus was not speaking of a literal, earthly treasure, but the eternal treasure which one finds through faith. The man's joy in finding the way to eternal happiness led him to "buy" the imaginary field (faith) and live an exemplary life in God that would lead him to an eternal reward. The undeveloped field is also important, for it represents the person barren of faith who is guided by the Holy Spirit and embraces God fully and without reservation.

A Pearl of a Buy (Matthew 13:47-50)

Similarly, in the pearl of great price, the merchant, undoubtedly experienced in such matters, finds a pearl, the likes of which he has never before seen. He sells everything he owns, knowing he might resell it at a much higher price than he paid for it. Again, this merchant's pearl was his finding faith and willing to sacrifice everything else to embrace it. His joy thus became inestimable, knowing he had found something far more valuable than an earthly asset.

The antithesis of this parable is found in Matthew (19:16-22). A rich young man approaches Jesus and asks how he can attain eternal life. He eagerly accepts the Lord's loving explanation but then his face falls when Jesus tells him to sell everything and follow him. Crestfallen, the young man goes away sad, unwilling to give up the riches he possesses. The siren call of earthly goods, for that man, was too much for him to ignore, no matter the price later on in life.

Following the man's departure, Jesus said to his disciples, "Again I say to you, it is easier for a camel to pass through the eye of a needle than for one who is rich to enter the kingdom of God." (Matthew: 19:24). This was a dramatic statement, emphasizing to the disciples that those who are consumed with riches and exclude all else are not going to enter the way to heaven, through the "narrow gate" (19:25).

Biblical scholars have offered speculation as to what Jesus meant when he said it is easier for a camel to pass through the eye of the needle than for a rich person to enter the eternal Kingdom (19:24). Most likely, he was referring to the needles at gates, through which people could pass, but not big animals, except with extreme difficulty. There have been other commentaries on this verse, but no general agreement as to its meaning. It is an unanswered question.

Section V – Feeding a Multitude

Bread and Fish for All (Matthew 14:13-21; Mark 6:31-44; Luke 9:12-17; John 6:1-14)

While not a parable, but rather a metaphor, the great miracles of feeding five thousand and then four thousand people on separate occasions had a dual purpose. They were: First, to satisfy the human need for food of all those who came to listen to Jesus, and second, to presage the Eucharist for the benefit, especially, of the disciples.

The second miracle, the Feeding of the 4,000, with seven loaves of bread and fish, is found Matthew (15:32-39) and Mark (8:1-9), but not in Luke or John (Wikipedia, online).

Though the disciples of Jesus questioned how they were to feed such a large throng, the Lord knew exactly what he was doing. Multiplying a tiny number of loaves and fish was more than providing a one-time meal; it was an important lesson to the Twelve that they were to feed everyone with something more than earthly food. They might not have perceived this at the time of the miracle, but they surely remembered it when Jesus sent them into the world to preach salvation, following his Resurrection.

Section VI – Parables of Reward and Punishment

The Net Snags Good and Not-So-Good (Matthew 13:47-50)

The theme in the seventh parable in Matthew is essentially similar to that of the wheat and weeds. A net cast into the sea catches fish of every kind. When the haul is brought to shore, the fishermen separate the good fish from the bad. Those they save are placed into buckets; the bad fish are thrown away.

Peter, Andrew, James and John, especially, would have related easily to this parable, having had significant experience on fishing boats in their careers as fishermen. The other disciples also would have been familiar with such a procedure, since fishing was a common occupation at the time of Jesus.

But the Lord did not stop at just saying the good fish are separated from the bad. He carried his message a telling step further, emphasizing to the disciples that the good fish gathered into a bucket are those who follow the word of God and lead worthy lives. The bad fish, conversely, are those who do not follow God's laws and are condemned. Jesus said emphatically, "Thus it will be at the end of the age. The angels will go out and separate the wicked from the righteous and throw them into the fiery furnace, where there will be the wailing and grinding of teeth" (13:49-50).

In the following verse (51), Jesus asked the disciples if the understood the meaning of that and the other preceding parables. Unanimously, they said "Yes." So, the Lord went ahead with an extension of the net parable, saying, that heaven is like the head of a household who brings to his living area both the new and the old. All people are to be offered the opportunity to attain salvation, whether they are new (people in our time) or old (those in Jesus' time). The Lord clearly meant that all human beings are offered God's grace, but only those who accept it and live by and in it will enjoy everlasting life.

As we go through this journey of uncovering deeper meanings in the parables, we will see some that provide a hope for salvation for one's good works, and also contain overt warnings by Jesus that those who hold grudges or do not forgive or help others is not the way to heaven. Perhaps one of the most dramatic parables emphasizing that theme is that of the unforgiving servant that follows

The disciple Peter, probably thinking he was being overly generous, approached Jesus one day and asked if he had to forgive someone as many as seven times. (In ancient Israel, forgiving someone three times was the norm.)

So, Peter was willing to forgive double-plus-one, not just three times. Jesus was quick to set the disciple straight: "I say to you not seven times, but seventy-seven times" (18:22). In other words, as many times as one is wronged. Forgiveness is to have no limit.

Be Unforgiving and Pay the Price! (Matthew 18:21-35)

Jesus followed that statement of forgiving others as many times as necessary with the parable of the unforgiving servant. In ancient times, servants were considered expendable and replaceable and were totally at the mercy of their masters, in this case, a king. We do not know in this parable how many servants owed the king for loans he had given them, only that there were more than one.

The servant of whom Jesus spoke owed so much money to the king that he could never possibly repay it. The king ordered the servant, his wife and children, to be sold, along with his property.

Once again, we find yet another example of God's infinite forgiveness. The king (God) gave forgiveness (grace for the forgiveness of sins) many times over to the servant, or sinner, deep in spiritual debt of sin. Past sins were forgiven, if the penitent was truly sorry. In the parable, that was not the case.

Stunned at the prospect of losing his family and never being able to pay back such a huge debt, the servant threw himself at the king's mercy and, indeed, was forgiven the debt by a most benevolent master (18:27). Lesson learned? Nope.

Despite being saved from a life of misery and deprivation and now possessing a fiendish sense of power, the servant immediately found another servant, who owed him a mere fraction of the debt for which he had been forgiven. Instead of using the spirit of human charity and telling the other servant he did not want repayment, this ingrate not only choked the other servant, but also then had him thrown into prison (18:28-30).

Unlike in the title of Shakespeare's play, "All's Well That Ends Well," such was not so for the unforgiving servant. Fearful, other of the king's servants went to him to report what they had just seen him do to a servant begging for mercy. The enraged king summoned the servant and had him thrown into prison. Because of the size of his debt, he likely would never see the light of day again (18:34). Jesus then warned, "So will my heavenly Father do to you, unless each of you forgives his brother from his heart" (18:35). No matter how difficult it might be to forgive someone who has seriously wronged us, it is the only way to inner peace and love.

God's forgiveness for any and all sins is limitless.

Don't Cross the Boss! Matthew (24:45-51), Mark (13:32-37), and Luke (12:25-40)

"When the cat is away, the mice will play." The parents of a teenager step out for the evening and warn their son or daughter not to have anyone over to the house. As soon as they leave, the teen is on the phone and a wild party begins. When the parents come home, and see the mess that awaits them, their teenager is not only punished – by being grounded or worse – but also is ordered to clean up everything.

Along the same lines, Jesus brought servants into his preaching in a similar scenario to the parable of the unfaithful servant. In Matthew's version, the household master puts one of his servants in charge of everything, to feed and care for others in the household. The servant does so and when the master returns from his journey is rewarded by being put in charge of all the master's property (Matthew 24:47).

Then, Jesus uses that same servant as not obedient, but wicked, thinking his master will be gone for a long time. Trying to take advantage of the master's absence, this servant beats his fellow servants and eats and drinks with drunkards. Unfortunately for him, the master returns unexpectedly (24:50-51). Whoops! Say goodbye, disloyal servant. Surely, he was sent packing to fend for himself.

In Mark, his shorter version has Jesus proclaiming much the same cautionary theme, but with a difference. The servants are all put in charge, and the gatekeeper is to be on the alert for the master's return. Jesus says it is important that the servants and gatekeeper must not be sleeping when the master returns unexpectedly (13:35-36). (See also the parable of the ten virgins, in which five sleep and are excluded from the wedding feast. So will those be excluded who are not alert to the presence of Jesus.)

Finally, Luke has Jesus blessing the vigilant servants, who open the door as soon as he arrives home from the wedding he has attended. As a reward, the master serves them a sumptuous meal and waits on them gratefully (13:37-38). If this role reversal by the master sounds a familiar ring, it should, for a similar scene is found in John's gospel (13:1-20), in which the Son of God humbles Himself and washes the disciples' feet. Peter, perhaps deeply shocked by the Master's action, objects, but Jesus quickly reminds that disciple that if he does not allow the Lord to wash his feet, "you will have no inheritance with me" (v.10). The Lord then emphasizes that his action is "...a model to follow, so that as I have done for you, you should also do" (13:15).

All three synoptic versions have the same meaning: Be alert, obey the laws of God, and treat others well and with love. Do not do evil things, for you never know when God will call you home to account for all your deeds during your lifetime.

As with the servant in Matthew's version, great rewards await those who are faithful to God and who do His holy will, but the opposite awaits those who ignore it and lead non-spiritual lives. Be awake always!

Nipsey Russell Would Have Approved (Luke 7:36-50)

Our next example of forgiveness involves not a servant – unforgiving or otherwise – but a Pharisee and a sinful woman. Again, God will forgive all sins; His love is endless for those who seek pardon.

The late comedian, Nipsey Russell, was one of the presenters at the Dean Martin roast of acerbic comedian Don Rickles in the 1970s. He said Rickles was at a Billy Graham revival where he (Rickles) supposedly said, "If you want to be forgiven for your sins, the first thing you have to do is sin!"

While Russell's statement was apocryphal and told in jest, a real-life example of forgiving a great sinner is the episode Luke recorded that is yet another instance of Jesus' command to forgive always. Simon the Pharisee had invited Jesus to a dinner at his home. During the meal, a sinful woman arrived and poured ointment over Jesus and then bathed his feet with her tears (7:38). It was not unusual for non-invited guests to enter a prominent person's home and observe silently what was being said. The sinful woman, however, entered for a vastly different reason.

Simon was upset and thought that Jesus should have known the woman was a grievous sinner. If he did not know this, then Jesus must not be a prophet. To be charitable, let us just say that Simon was a bit naïve or obtuse regarding the stature of his special guest.

Being God, Jesus read Simon's mind and posed a question to him in the form of a parable. As in the parable of the unforgiving servant, two men owed money to a creditor – five hundred days' wages for one of the men, and fifty for the other. As the king in the other parable forgave the servant who owed an enormous amount, the creditor wrote off the debt both men had incurred. Jesus than asked Simon which of the two debtors would love the creditor more. Simon correctly said that the man owing much more would also love much more (7:43).

Having proved a point to Simon, Jesus then gently reminded his host that he did not give him water for his feet or greet him with a kiss. Nor did the host anoint his guest with oil – standard procedures in ancient Israel to show respect for the guest (7:44).

As a Pharisee, Simon should have accorded such a greeting, since Pharisees were strict observers of the law and social procedures. But the Lord was not chastising Simon for violating social protocol. Rather, he was pointing out that the sinful woman deliberately sacrificed a jar of expensive ointment as she sought Jesus' forgiveness for her sins. This woman showed more faith in the Lord than Simon, who was hung up on being too rigid toward sinful people, when he might have showed a modicum of understanding in the spirit of charity.

Jesus told Simon the woman's many sins were forgiven, because she loved much. Simon did not have such a big heart, resulting in the Lord saying, "So I tell you, her many sins have been forgiven; hence, she has shown great love. But the one to whom little is forgiven, loves little" (7:47). It was a Divine "Take that, Simon!" Did that Pharisee learn his lesson? We will never know, but Jesus opened wide the door to Simon to change his life in a way that would be much more likely to earn him a place in heaven.

Section VII – Be Prepared (Not Only
for Boy and Girl Scouts!)

The motto of the Boy Scouts and Girl Scouts is, "Be prepared." That is great advice not only for those involved in scouting, but also for any of us. Jesus stressed this in different ways, but always with the same moral. The following parable could not be clearer in how important it is to anticipate, at all times, the Lord's arrival for us and our judgment.

For Lack of a Wedding Garment... (Matthew 22:1-14)

Everyone loves to attend a wedding and celebrate that special day with the bride and groom. Even in today's trend toward more casual dressing, men and women alike dress up in appropriate garments and then journey to join in the Sacrament at church, and then go to the reception for a joyous celebration.

Matthew's depiction of the parable of the wedding feast might seem to convey a rather bizarre message. Why would Jesus have a wedding guest show up without proper attire and be roughly treated by being cast out of the wedding hall? On the surface, this might seem to be cruel and uncalled for, but there is more to the Lord's message than it would appear.

In this parable, a king who wanted to have a great wedding celebration for his son. He, of course, invited relatives, friends and others well ahead of the occasion. Unfortunately, many made excuses and some even murdered the servants sent to extend them an invitation. The enraged king then sent his army to kill those murderers and burn their city (22:5-7). This seems a bit extreme, especially preceding such a joyous event, but kings at that time had immense powers and could commit such acts with impunity.

The king, incensed beyond belief, then ordered his servants to go out and collect all whom they find and bring them to the wedding feast. It would seem that this was a last-minute decision, but even so, the wedding hall was quickly filled with guests, all of whom were dressed appropriately. So, how did one guest stick out like the proverbial sore thumb because he did not appear in a wedding garment?

In those times, it was often a custom to hand out wedding garments as guests arrived, or at least give them plenty of notice that the feast was ready. So, while it might seem as if the newly invited guests were immediately brought to the wedding hall, in reality they all had time to at least change clothes or, if already in clean garments (acceptable in ancient Israel), go directly to the feast. It is likely the man without a wedding garment might well have had a soiled garment (as seen in the rabbinic parable earlier in this work), which would be an insult to the wedding host and his family. It is also possible he was not offered a wedding garment because he was a late arrival and no more were at hand. (For details on this custom, see Bible Commentaries.com/Matthew 22.)

What is the message here? The king is God, who invites everyone to eternal life. Those who refuse the Creator's invitation are condemned because of their refusal to accept the need to lead a good life and go their sinful way. Those sent to invite others after the original guests declined the king's invitation are the disciples, who were charged with preaching the gospel and gathering souls for the Kingdom. Still, even with the repentant souls – represented by the new wedding guests – there is one unrepentant sinner at hand. He is not to be admitted to the Kingdom but must be cast outside into the darkness (hell). Jesus warned, "Many are invited, but few are chosen" (22:14). The "wedding garment" is the cloak of repentance, and we must wear it at all times if we are to be invited to the unending feast that is heaven.

More Ungrateful Invitees (Luke 14:16-24)

Speaking of banquets, Luke describes one in which circumstances are quite similar to those in the preceding parable. Jesus told this parable while a guest for dinner at a prominent Pharisee's home. The main difference in this parable is that a man (not a king) wants to honor his friends and others with a great feast. However, all the invited guests refuse to come. This was extremely rude to the host, as it was to the king in our other parable.

Unlike the king, this man did not order his troops (if he even had any) to kill those who refused to attend and burn their city. Yes, he flew into a justified rage, but he then ordered his servants to go out and bring to the feast "...the poor and the crippled, the blind and the lame" (14:22).

The servants did as ordered, but then told their master there was still room for the master told the servants to go out and "make people come in that my home will be filled. For, I tell you, none of those men who were invited will taste of my dinner" (14:23-24).

It could not be clearer that Jesus was letting his listeners know that salvation was for all, not a select few. However, he also was letting them know that those who did not listen to the Lord's call for repentance and acceptance of faith would not be part of the Kingdom. The Lord came to save the lost souls of Israel, but only those who listened to the gospel and heeded it would be saved.

Lamps Light the Way – Sometimes (Matthew 25:1-13)

Perhaps the basic question in this parable is, why did five virgins – bridesmaids – take enough oil for their lamps, and five did not come prepared for the bridegroom's arrival? Well, we can deduce that the bridegroom was definitely arriving at the wedding hall at night. Otherwise, no lamps would have been needed. The five foolish virgins might not have anticipated the bridegroom's delay and took a chance his arrival would be earlier. So, they thought they would not need extra oil for their lamps.

Alas, they erred, but not on the side of caution. All ten virgins grew tired as they waited for the bridegroom. One reason for his being delayed could have been because he was making last-minute arrangements or agreements with his future in-laws, or, perhaps there were a few details left to iron out before the wedding. Since, in ancient Israel, an entire village might be invited to a wedding, glitches of many kinds could arise at the last minute.

When the bridegroom finally made his way to the banquet hall, shouts of his arrival shook the virgins from their slumber. The five foolish virgins were suddenly dismayed, because their lamps were short of oil. The other five virgins, who had indeed prepared well by bringing extra oil, were not being selfish when they refused to share some of their oil, since they knew they needed enough oil to light the bridegroom's way into the wedding hall (25:6-9).

At that point in the parable, is a subtle symbolism. The virgins were lighting the way for the bridegroom. The lamps represented the light of Christ, the bridegroom, who was to bring His light to the world for all to follow. The fact that five had enough to light the way and five did not means some follow Jesus to a path leading to the unending light, while others let the darkness of a lack of faith envelop them.

Going to the merchant to buy oil That part of the parable can be seen as depicting pe late at night also has significance. People who stray from the way to eternal life live in the darkness. When they do come to their senses and realize how foolish they really were, it is too late and the door to heaven is closed forever. Conversely, to those who carry the light from the lamp of faith, that same door is always open.

The Servant Who Dug Himself a Hole – Literally (Matthew 25:14-30; Luke 19:11-27)

Laziness never leads to a reward, and there is no better example of this than the hapless servant in the parable of the talents, another one in which Jesus emphasized the need to be prepared as he did in the parable of the ten virgins. The Lord addressed this parable, as well as the preceding one, to the twelve disciples. There are two versions of this parable. The first is in Matthew 25:14-30; the second is in Luke 19:11-27). Both gospel writers place the parable just before the entry into Jerusalem and show they were intended to both encourage and caution the disciples regarding the mission to which they would be entrusted following Jesus' death and resurrection.

Here we have the master of a household who entrusts a goodly sum of money to three of his servants. To one he gives five talents, to the second two talents, and to the third one talent, each according to the level of how hard they work for him and how trustworthy they are. He then departs and goes on a journey.

Before we continue looking at the meaning of this parable, a bit of explanation is necessary. At the time of Jesus, a talent was worth about twenty years of wages for an average worker, so the first servant was entrusted with approximately one hundred years of wages, the second with forty years, and the third twenty years. (See also Carla Works, Commentary on Matthew 25:14-30, at workingpreacher.org.)

Surely, this amount of money must have shaken the servants, even the one with just one talent. Nonetheless, the other two were more ambitious than the third and invested their master's money. The third dug a hole and buried the talent, probably figuring he was doing the right thing or was simply afraid of severe punishment if he somehow lost the talent through bad investments. Little did he know!

When the master returned he naturally wanted an accounting from his servants as to how well they invested his money. (He must have been on a very long journey for the interest on the money to have doubled with the investments made by two of the servants.) Pleased that the first two servants had doubled their master's talents, the boss conferred considerable control and responsibilities on both. In doing so, he made them both very wealthy for being so willing to be good and trustworthy (25:23).

Alas, the third did nothing that the master wished. He approached him with excuses, trying to justify his lack of action by reminding the master that he was demanding and capable of succeeding without trying. The servant then handed his master the coin and might even have awaited plaudits. His "reward" instead was to be fired and expelled from the household forever (25:30).

Yes, that servant, and maybe the other two, feared their master, who must have been very strict in his ways. Yet, he alone did not follow the lead of the other servants by investing the talent. His badly misplaced reasoning and laziness cost him his livelihood and future.

This parable was a pointed message to the disciples that they were to be charged with not only believing in Jesus, but also through preaching, baptizing, and in other ways bringing others into the Faith. They were entrusted with spiritual "talents" and were to double – at least – their "money" throughout their lives in the Holy Name. Then, they would hear echoes of Jesus' words in the parable where he had the master saying, "Well done, my good and faithful servant…Come share your master's joy" (25:23). Amen!

As we look at a similar parable in Luke (19:11-27), we see there are significant differences. In Luke's version, Jesus was at the house of Zacchaeus, a local tax collector. Jesus told the parable to the assembled guests, rather than the disciples.

Both versions, however, have a common thread of preparedness and reward and punishment. The master in Matthew's version was now presented in Luke as a nobleman who is going on a journey to claim a kingship. Instead of three servants, this nobleman had ten gold coins and divided them with each one. Further, the nobleman gave explicit instructions to the ten servants to "engage in trade with them until I return" (19:13). While Matthew's account does not mention such an order, the fact that two of the servants engaged in trade shows an implicit order to trade, using the entrusted coins.

When the master returned from his journey, he called for an accounting of the servants' success – or lack of it. Here, things become a little confusing, because only three of the ten are asked how well they did. The first servant proudly reported he doubled the number of coins with which he was entrusted. The servant with five coins also said he doubled the number of coins. As in the Matthean version, the third servant told his master that he feared him because of his being so demanding, so he wrapped the one coin he was given and dutifully handed it back to the master (19:19-21).

The nobleman rewarded the first servant with taking charge of ten cities, and the second with five cities. As for the third servant, Luke did not have him being cast out, but the master severely chastised him and took away the gold coin to give to the servant with ten.

How did the parable go from ten servants receiving gold coins to just three? The number is unimportant. Here is what Jesus was conveying to Zacchaeus and all others at the dinner: To those who are entrusted with the gift of faith, the more they practice their faith and share it to help others grow in spirituality, the more will be their heavenly reward.

Pope Francis emphasized this, commenting on this parable: "Through this parable our Lord teaches us that, although his reign has begun, it will only be fully manifested later on. In the time left to us we should use all the resources and graces God gives us, in order to merit the reward" (Pope Francis on the Parable of the Gold Coins, at catholicsstrivingforholiness.org).

In other words, to those hearing Jesus thought the Kingdom of God was coming soon. In reality the Lord was telling his listeners that the more faith one has, the more reward will be given. The less faith one has, more will be taken away. It was a sobering, yet inspiring message.

Now, there is another "hidden" message in Luke's parable. Verse 14 reveals that the nobleman, who was seeking a kingship, was despised by citizens of that city. After he began his journey, some of them sent a delegation to whoever was going to confer kingship on him, saying they did not want him as their king. Was that an interruption in the parable? Not at all.

We need only to remind ourselves that Jesus was despised by the Jewish leaders, who rejected him as the Messiah. When Jesus included this statement in the Lukan account of the parable, he meant it as a prelude to his own rejection, suffering and death at the hands of those who despised and rejected him. At the end of this parable (19:27), the newly named king orders those who rejected him to be slain before his eyes. Symbolically, this referred to those condemned to eternal punishment who reject and hate the Redeemer.

Section VIII – Be Rich in Faith, not Material Goods

Barns Hold Wheat, not Eternal Rewards (Luke 12:16-21)

Often, Jesus used remarks by listeners to make a telling point. Here is one such result, while the Lord was addressing yet another one of his crowds in response to what a voice in the crowd was calling out.

Someone in a gathering demanded that Jesus tell his brother to share the family inheritance with him. The lord knew the speaker was acting out of personal greed and immediately rejected the man's personal-gain demand. Further, Jesus let everyone there that day understand that earthly riches are but temporary; spiritual riches are forever. He said: "Take care to guard against all greed, for though one may be rich, one's life do said to him, does not consist of possessions" (13:15).

This brings us to the parable of the rich fool. Jesus presented a man who had such a bountiful harvest that he had to build new barns to store all his wheat and whatever else he might have grown. Congratulating himself, the man said he would eat, drink and be merry for the rest of his life. Well, he might have enjoyed a last meal and wine, but that night God called him home for an accounting of his greed. Jesus warned, "Thus it will be for the one who stores up treasure for himself, but into rich in what matters to God" (12:21).

Rich Man, Poor Man (Luke 16:19-31)

Here is a parable of dramatic contrast between rich and poor people. It is one of two instances in which Jesus make it abundantly clear that eternal damnation awaits those who do not share what has been granted to them in life with those who have much less.

The parable of Lazarus and the (unnamed) rich man has a unique feature. Is the only one of Jesus' parables in which someone is named. This parable is a strict and dark reminder that greed and hoarding of riches ultimately lead to a soul's destruction. It is disturbing, yet as we examine the parable, we see it also offers at least a hint of hope.

The scene Jesus set could, with updating, parallel the social issues of today's life. It pits the rich against the poor, and the haves versus the have-nots. Most important, the parable is a grim reminder that riches and the love of them lead only to a tragic end.

A rich man sat in his luxurious home, dressed in fine purple garments (a mark of wealth in ancient Israel), and wined and dined sumptuously every day of his life. While he undoubtedly was aware of Lazarus' presence just outside his front door, he did not lift a finger to help this poor man.

Jesus painted Lazarus as being super-poor, one of the invisible people at the lowest rung of society. In total contrast to the luxurious life of the rich man, he was dressed in rags or worn clothing and was suffering from sores all over his body caused at least somewhat by the coarse garments he wore. His lot was akin to homeless people who wander aimlessly on streets today.

Compounding Lazarus' ills were the dogs who came and licked his sores. He was a miserably deprived human being, for sure. Yet, when this poor man died, he was granted eternal life. Conversely, the rich man also died and was condemned to the eternal flames of hell (16:22).

What is the message here? Of course, love of riches by the wealthy man is at the forefront and needs no explanation, but his real downfall was more than that. It stemmed from his ignoring another human being who longed for even scraps from the rich man's table, but who received none. The rich man was so consumed by his sumptuous lifestyle (just as was the homeowner who thought his bountiful harvest would bring him years of wining and dining) that he totally ignored the plight of those who had almost nothing.

We tend to think that people of means are selfish and full of themselves. While that might be true in some people, other wealthy people start and fund foundations, give away millions of dollars to charities, and help make lives better for those who are less fortunate.

On the other hand, we tend to feel that poor people are always to be pitied and are good souls. Who is to say that some homeless or other less-fortunate people are not seething with hatred and rage and wishing bad things for those of means? Both views are never one hundred percent true, but in this parable Jesus gives us a dramatic contrast between the rich man and the beggar, as well as the necessity for helping those in dire need.

We can conclude that, despite his wretched lot in life, Lazarus was, at the core of his heart, a loving person and one of deep faith. Otherwise, he would not have been saved for heaven. The rich man, however, committed a grievous sin of omission – he simply did not care about anyone else, including those in need.

There is a little underlying symbolism in this parable. Note that the poor man, resting peacefully in heaven, did not speak. He was totally comforted and infinitely joyous because his lifelong suffering had been replaced by forever happiness. He was in God's presence and had no need to say a single word.

Aha, but the rich man now realized the error of his ways and tried to make his case with Abraham. Why was Abraham the one cuddling Lazarus? Because he was the father of the Jewish nation, and Jesus' audience of Pharisees and others would have absorbed the strong message the Lord delivered. Abraham strove to show the Nation of Israel that God wished all to leads worthy lives, so they could enjoy eternal happiness. Jesus was strongly conveying that those who embrace worldly things and do not care about others will suffer tragic consequences.

Now, for the first time, the rich man knew he had done no good for Lazarus and perhaps many others. Far too late, he realized the errors of his ways and wanted the formerly poor man to help him, thinking that if Lazarus could even lessen his suffering by giving him water, his sufferings would be lessened (16:24). It was not to be, as Abraham gently reminded him that he had everything he wanted in life, while Lazarus had nothing but poverty and hopelessness.

Abraham also noted that there is an insurmountable gulf between heaven and hell, and no one can ever cross from one to the other. Still hoping to lessen his torments, the rich man begged Abraham to send Lazarus to his father's house and warn his five brothers of the dire consequences for being selfish and uncaring (16:27-28). We might see this as being a family affair of greed, for why else would the condemned man want to caution his brothers? Were they also part of the carefree wining, dining and non-caring days? Quite possibly, they were so involved.

In the conclusion of this parable, Jesus imparted a statement to the Pharisees concerning their lack of belief in him. Abraham rejected the rich man's plea to send Lazarus as a warning to his brothers. Jesus issued his own warning to the Pharisees that presages how they would react to his own death, through Abraham: "If they will not listen to Moses and the prophets, neither will they be persuaded if someone should rise from the dead" (16:31).

As we know only too well, that is exactly what transpired – and continues to this day. Faith is the greatest gift to us, and those who reject it do so at the risk of losing their immortal souls.

The Sheep (Baa) and the Goats (Blah)
(Matthew 25:31-46)

In the preceding parable, Jesus sent a stern warning to his listeners that not caring and ignoring the plight of those who are in need can very well lead to a bad and eternal end. His parable of the sheep and the goats presents an even more dire warning, but also promises eternal life to those who do good deeds and who love God. We saw much the same theme in the parable of the talents (Matthew 25:14-30) and the gold coins (Luke 19:11-27). Those who followed the will of the master (God) and expanded faith beyond themselves were rewarded, while those who did little were severely punished.

In Matthew, the parable of the separation of the sheep and the goats follows that of the talents, while in Luke, the entry into Jerusalem immediately follows the parable of the gold coins (19:28-40). Both gospel writers were keenly focused on the eschatological aspects of all three of these reward/punishment parables.

This begs the question as to why Jesus used the analogy of sheep and goats for this, his boldest of all reward/punishment statements. Why did he not just say good people and bad people? The answer is found in the natures of those two animals. Sheep, as noted elsewhere in this work, are gentle animals who obey the commands of the shepherd, whose voice they always recognize and obey. They are non-aggressive and cannot easily be stirred to anger. It is why Jesus called himself the Good Shepherd, subtly showing the disciples and others that he loved his sheep (us) without qualification. We are all part of his flock.

Goats, however, have some negative characteristics. They tend to be messy, aggressive and not at all obedient to their master. Regardless of whether they eat tin cans – as they are sometimes portrayed doing –

their behavior can be the polar opposite of what we see in sheep. Also, they are not noted to be gentle. Pet one at your own risk!!

Jesus' memorable point in this parable was to prepare those hearing his words to what lay ahead for them for all eternity. Do well and you will be with God forever. Do bad and you will never see God at all.

Perhaps the most uplifting aspect to this parable is the Lord's laying out the key to salvation in a way that is so wonderfully simple to follow. People who do good deeds and do not seek credit for them become the sheep of the parable. Feed the hungry, visit the sick, clothe those who lack clothes, welcome those who need human kindness, and perform other works of charity, and salvation awaits you (25:37-39).

Notice Jesus did not call for us to do extraordinary works, just those little acts of kindness that help others enjoy a better life. Contributing to a charity that helps less-fortunate people, paying for someone else's groceries when you see they are struggling at the cashier's station in the supermarket, donating good clothing, sitting and talking with a stranger, or providing solace to someone who has experienced a tragic loss are just a few of the ways to be in God's loving grace. It is not at all difficult.

Let us not dwell on the fate of the "goats." As Jesus warned, those who do not do good things for others must pay the full price. Like the rich man who could not have cared less about Lazarus, those who ignore the needs of others deliberately are sealing their own doom. Reaching out to help others is so easy and rewarding. Go for it!

Now, here is the quintessential parable on how helping friends, neighbors or total strangers makes us better and stronger people.

Section IX – Love and Help for All

Forever the Good Samaritan (Luke 10:29-37)

From the time Jesus delivered the parable of the Good Samaritan until our present day, people who reach out to others in serious need are called Good Samaritans. That is all well and good, but does that mean Samaritans were otherwise bad people? To understand why the term became a forever part of vocabularies around the world, a brief explanation is in order.

Samaria was the capital of the Kingdom of Israel and comprised the ten northern tribes. They were fully in accord with all Jewish traditions, including those of the Southern Kingdom (which was called Judah). That all ended in the year 721 B.C., when the Assyrians overran the Northern Kingdom and brought their people there to settle in Samaria and the surrounding areas. (See The Second Book of Kings, chapters 17 and 18 for details on both the Assyrian takeover and its subsequent actions.)

Because of inter-marrying and other influences of the Assyrian occupation – including worship of idols – the tribes of the Northern Kingdom became a separate religious sect and stopped following the laws and rites of the Jews. Thus, the tribes in the Southern Kingdom shunned those in the north and had nothing whatever to with them.

Jesus was not bound by inhumanities by others, though he was once not welcomed in a Samaritan village, because he was traveling to Jerusalem and the Samaritans wanted nothing to do with anyone heading to that city. Not coincidentally, it was that rejection which previewed the final rejection in Jerusalem by the Pharisees and other Jewish leaders and his subsequent arrest and crucifixion. Disciples

James and John, furious that their Master was told to leave the Samaritan village, wanted the Lord to call down fire from heaven on that place (Luke 9:54). They were not happy when Jesus rebuked them sharply, reminding them in his own way that love and forgiveness, not wrath, are the way to win hearts and minds.

What James and John wanted Jesus to do had a precedent in 2 Kings 1:9-15. The prophet Elijah refused to obey the command of King Ahaziah, who had fallen and injured himself. The king ordered a captain and fifty of his men to seek the man (Elijah) who had turned aside the king's messengers. That was because Ahaziah wanted to know if the god, Baalzebub, would let him recover. The first troops who approached Elijah were consumed by fire from heaven. So were all those in the second contingent sent by the king. Elijah was making it known in the most dramatic way that he was a man of the true, living God not a false god. The third contingent's captain begged Elijah to spare him and his men, and an angel told the prophet it was all right to go to the king. Unfortunately for Ahaziah, Elijah revealed to him that he was to die immediately, and he did. Belief in a false god was the king's fatal mistake.

Jesus showed absolutely no need to call down fire for being shunned. If those in the Samaritan village did not want him, he would seek believers elsewhere. Note that he did not condemn the villagers. Forgiveness is always something Jesus held out, and still does, to everyone.

So, let us see why Jesus used the despised (to the Jews) Samaritans as examples of being true believers. The parable of the Good Samaritan (Luke 10:29-36) not only depicts a person of great compassion, but also shows how Jesus could provide a lesson to a skeptic and teach him the true meaning of human relations.

An unnamed scholar of the law, upon hearing Jesus' command to love not only God, but also neighbors, condescendingly sneered at those words and asked, "And who is my neighbor?" (10:29). He said this to justify himself, but was totally unprepared for the Lord's response, in the form of a parable, that quickly followed.

Traveling alone from Jerusalem to Jericho, a man was set upon by robbers who were not content just to steal his money or goods. After robbing him, they beat him and left him helpless and half-dead by the side of the road. A priest and Levite saw the victim but chose to cross to the other side of the road without lifting a finger to help. Then, a Samaritan came down the road and not only stopped, but also dressed the man's wounds, put him on his animal, and then entrusted him to an innkeeper, paying for the man's stay before he continued on his journey.

It might seem there is little to interpret here, but the Lord's parables always had messages that lay beneath the surface. This one is no exception.

We might shake our heads upon learning that two Jewish spiritual leaders ignored someone in dire need, and we would be correct in that view. The priest and Levite knew if they so much as touched the wounded man they would render themselves ritually impure and would have to be banned from conducting their duties for the time prescribed by Mosaic Law. That might be the reason they crossed the road.

In terms of human compassion, however, those two spiritual leaders committed a sin of omission. Becoming ritually impure was a temporary situation. Coming to the aid of a dying man should have superseded that consideration. To this day, both men are representative of those who ignore others for their own needs, selfish or otherwise.

The Samaritan, however, had an entirely different mindset. He got off the animal on which he was riding, poured oil over the victim's wounds, and carried him to a nearby inn, where he cared for him. Departing the next day, he entrusted the man's care to the innkeeper and paid in advance for the man's lodging. He further trusted that the innkeeper would indeed provide care for the wounded man.

He might or might not have thought that, once he was out of sight, that the innkeeper would put the man out. Innkeepers in ancient Israel were often not the most honest of businesspeople, so the Samaritan was taking a calculated risk. Yes, but it was much deeper than that. It was a huge act of faith! We can see the innkeeper as God and man as a believer. By placing the man in God's hands, the Samaritan showed the greatest act of mercy and human kindness possible.

We can only wonder how humbled that scholar of the law became after listening to the wonderfully instructive lesson Jesus taught him. Too bad he did not know a rather humorous modern-day expression, in which an anonymous person asked, "If we are here to help others, why are the others here?" The answer is that we all must be Samaritans in spirit and never cease to help others. It is our great Christian contribution to God and our fellow man.

A Friend in Need is to be Helped (Luke 11:5-8)

There is an old saw that says a friend in need is a friend in deed. It is true, for when we help others in need, they will reciprocate when we, too, have an important need. A friend in need is actually, like the victim in the preceding parable, one to whom we should give of ourselves willingly and without thought for being reciprocated by that person. So it is with the unusual theme of the parable of the friend at midnight.

Be honest – how would we feel if someone rang our doorbell at midnight and said they just had someone arrive unexpectedly and needed food for the guest? Being so interrupted from a sound sleep certainly would not be exactly good for neighborly relations. Our initial reaction, after we knew it was a good friend or a close neighbor, would be the same as the homeowner in the parable: "Do not bother me; the door has already been locked and my children and I already in bed. I cannot get up to give you anything" (11:7).

Geez, what a grouch! However, who could blame him? Yet, the homeowner did accommodate his neighbor. As Jesus said, it was not because of friendship, but rather because of his neighbor's persistence (11:8). That is why Jesus emphasized immediately after that parable, that if you ask God you will receive, seek and you will find (faith), and knock (ask God to love you) and the door will open (11:9). Enhanced spirituality is always yours, for as Jesus said following the parable, "…how much more will the Father in heaven give the holy Spirit to those who ask him" (11:13). After all the Holy Spirit is not only the Third Person of the Holy Trinity, but also the Lord and Giver of Life.

Section X – Lost and Found Department

We now turn to a trilogy of parables that emphasize what is lost through sin can be found through grace and love. Our first two are that of the lost sheep and the lost coin Our third is the longest of all parables of Jesus, the Prodigal Son.

Joy over Finding a Lost Sheep (Luke 15:4-7)

We learn, once again, the scribes and Pharisees were complaining about Jesus, saying he welcomed and ate with sinners. We can almost hear the Lord sighing after having heard that baseless complaint so many times from those Jewish spiritual leaders. And, once again, the Lord patiently let those doubters know what true love and forgiveness are all about.

Being a shepherd was a common occupation in ancient Israel, so the parable's theme would have been abundantly clear to Jesus' listeners. In fact, some might have been landowners with sheep themselves, since Jesus began this parable by saying, "What man among you having a hundred sheep and losing one of them would not leave the ninety-nine…" (15:4). Thus, the shepherd would seek the lost sheep and not rest until he found it and returned it, on his shoulders, to the flock (15:5).

Is there not a message of great trust in this parable? Once the shepherd sought the lost sheep, he somehow knew the others in the flock would not run away. And once he found the stray he would ask his friends and neighbors to rejoice with him, because the lost sheep had been found.

Of course, the Lord's main idea he imparted to his listeners was that the ninety-nine sheep were those souls who were saved forever in heaven. The stray sheep was a person who had abandoned the faith and gone his or her own way, but in the end repented and was brought back into the eternal flock. That was why the Lord said there will be more joy in heaven when a sinner repents than for the ninety-nine pious souls who no longer needed to repent.

Help! Where is My Coin? (Luke 15:8-10)

Have you ever lost something and looked frantically for it everywhere without success? You mention this to a friend or relative who might ask, "Where did you lose it?" Irritated and frustrated, your answer might well be, "If I knew that, I would know where to find it!"

In the parable of the lost coin, Jesus did not mention anything like the above, but he emphasized that the woman who lost the coin diligently lit a lamp and swept the house from stem to stern until she retrieved that lost coin (15:8). Probably not a woman of great means, she needed every cent for buying food and other necessities. That was why she was so persistent in finding the one coin she has misplaced.

As in the parable of the lost sheep, Jesus emphasized it was more than a coin that was lost; it was a falling away from faith. The woman represented a repentant sinner who sought God fervently, and after much tribulation found Him and rejoiced. Her friends and neighbors, already people of faith, rejoiced with her. Jesus repeated what he said in the parable of the lost sheep: "…there will be rejoicing among the angels of God over one sinner who repents" (15:10).

A "Dead" Son Comes Back to Life (Luke 15:11-32)

Our final parable in the "lost and found" trilogy is the longest of all parables, and for good reason – it is the strongest possible message of God's mercy and forgiveness. No one who sins and seeks God's forgiveness will ever be banned from eternal life.

Most young people are idealistic and have dreams as to what they want to do in life for personal success and to help others. Some, however, let their dreams turn into nightmares. The green grass they see on the other side of the fence eventually turns brown. It was so for the young man in this parable.

The young man demanding his half of the family inheritance definitely was lured to the "good life", perhaps not wanting to be burdened by the responsibilities of working in the family's fields. It was not the wisest choice, as he soon discovered.

In an unusual move, when this errant lad asked for his share of the family fortune, the father granted his request. Looking beyond the fact of splitting the inheritance with his two sons, the father represents God, who imparted free will to all human beings. While he foresaw what was going to happen to the young man, he nonetheless let him go off to a distant land (sin). Loving or not loving God is the free will the Creator instills in our human spirit. The choices are always ours.

Things did not turn out so well for this happy-go-lucky young man. Not only did he squander all the money his father had given him, he also found himself in dire need when a great famine overcame the country in which he had settled (15:14). The "green grass" he thought was the key to a great life had turned brown.

Here, the famine represents a spiritually barren soul – the consequence of turning from God. It can also be said to symbolize the fate of the entire country to which this young man had journeyed. There is a subtle hint from Jesus to that effect. If the prodigal son had been attracted to the dissolute life in that land, it is not beyond reason to believe that most of the people living there had abandoned God for amorality or simply not caring about faith.

Though others in the country were also suffering from the great famine, the young man, scared and reluctant to return to his father's house, was in dire need. Desperate and frantic, he found a job of sorts – tending the swine of a local farmer (15:15). This was one of the most demeaning tasks possible. Worse, if the young man was part of a Jewish family, he was involved in a job that rendered him unclean. Even eating the pods he fed to those animals were considered unclean by the Jews (Opusdei.org, online).

Realizing the horrible mistake he had made and the disgrace he had brought to his father, the errant son did some serious thinking. He thought, why, my father's servants have more than enough to eat, but no one here gives me anything (15:17). How stupid and senseless have I been!

In recalling the servants, the young man realized those who do not stray from the love of God have all the bread they want and never go hungry. Why did Jesus specifically use bread for the young man's thoughts? Once again, the Lord was hinting of the coming of the Bread of Life, the Eucharist. The faithful can always satisfy their spiritual hunger through the Body and Blood of our Savior.

Having realized he needed to not only return home, but also ingratiate himself to his father, the younger son concocted a statement of what he wanted to say to his father upon his arrival home: "Father, I have sinned against heaven and against you. I no longer deserve to be called your son; treat me as you would treat One of your hired workers"

(15:19). One might say he was an ancient public relations practitioner, but in reality he was genuinely fearful of rejection and condemnation from his father.

That was not to be, however. This man's father had never ceased looking out from a high point in his house day after day, hoping and praying fervently that his lost son would someday return. This was God, always looking for lost souls to return to the flock, where He could welcome them back, no questions asked, and embrace them forever. The return of the prodigal son to his family resulted in instant and unending forgiveness. The sinner had repented and was truly sorry. God never ceases to forgive.

Such was not the case with the older son, who boiled over with anger when he learned from the servants his younger son was back and the joy of music and feasting was carrying the day. Whether it was jealousy or just deep resentment, the older brother wanted no part of the festivities. He reminded his father that he had been loyal but had never been granted any special favors. It was then his father reminded him that he would inherit the estate one day, but there must be rejoicing, for the lost child had returned (15:28-30).

The older son lost nothing, for he was the one who never left the flock and did his father's (God's) bidding. He was spiritually secure. The younger brother had died to God, but then repented of all those serious sins. He had, indeed, come back to life in the Spirit (15:32).

One Son Listened; One Did Not (Matthew 21:28-32)

Getting children, especially teenagers, to help with the chores, can often be an exasperating issue in a parent's life. Just in case you might have thought this is a recent phenomenon or problem, we know it actually dates far back in history. It might well be why Jesus chose to use obedience in the form of a parable to the chief priests and elders.

That day, those Jewish religious leaders had questioned Jesus as to by what authority he had to teach. They did so because they knew the Lord did not study under rabbis earlier in his life.

To answer their question, Jesus put their feet to the fire and asked whether John's baptism was from human or divine origin. After they discussed this among themselves, they admitted to Jesus they did not know. So, he said, "Neither shall I tell you by what authority I do these things" (21:25-27).

But Jesus did not simply dismiss the leaders and their questions. He seized the opportunity to relate a brief parable aimed directly at them. It involved a vineyard, a man and his two sons.

The father told one son to go work in the vineyard, but the son said he would not do so. Talk about disobedience and arrogance! However, the son changed his mind and obeyed his father's wish. Then, the father told his other son to go work in the vineyard, and that lad said he would, but did not go. So, Jesus asked an obvious question that even the assembled leaders could answer: "Which of the two did his father's will?" The leaders answered, "The first" (21:31).

Though their answer was correct, Jesus did not let them off the hook. He excoriated the chief priests and elders for not believing John the Baptist, and further did not believe John even after tax collectors and prostitutes did (21:32). Jesus was referring not only to John, but also to himself, for the Jewish leaders rejected his teaching at every opportunity. Little wonder their disbelief led to their condemning the Lord and having him put to death. The second of the two sons represented the leaders to whom Jesus addressed that parable, showing that disbelief and disobedience both have negative consequences.

Section XI – Unhappy Workers, an Unjust Judge, a Dishonest Steward, and an Arrogant Pharisee

Workers Who Cried "Foul"! (Matthew 20:1-16)

Some workers are satisfied with their lot; others are unhappy for one reason or another. The workers in the vineyard is an example of how all who labor for God during their lifetime will be handsomely rewarded with eternal life, even if they are late to the Faith.

We might come away after reading this parable agreeing with the workers who were hired first but then grumbled when they did not receive additional pay at the end. After all, they reminded the owner of the vineyard, they toiled under the hot sun all day, while those hired last scarcely did anything at all. Yes, by today's procedures, it would seem fair to either give the first workers more and the last ones less, but that was not the point Jesus was trying to make to his disciples when he told this parable. The moral was also an important lesson to the Twelve that coming to love God can happen at any time in a person's life. And he or she will enjoy the same reward as those who embraced faith earlier in their life.

Note that Jesus had the owner of the vineyard telling his foreman to summon the last workers first and the first ones last. This was to be repeated at the end of the parable as an exclamation point, to hammer home the lesson. We can sympathize with the workers who toiled all day and endured harsh weather conditions, but as the vineyard owner (a.k.a. Jesus) told them, "What if I wish to give this last one the same as you?...Are you envious because I am generous?" (20:14-15) As Jesus reminded the Twelve by way of this parable, "Thus, the last will be first and the first will be last" (20: 16).

The point of the Lord's parable was that it does not matter if someone is faithful all his or her life, doing good things, worshipping God every day, or someone who has rejected the Creator then, later in life, finds faith and atones for sins. The Lord welcomes everyone who loves him, even those who come to him last. All are entitled to the same eternal reward.

Here Comes the (Not-so-Just) Judge Luke 18:1-8).

In an earlier discussion, we saw a man knocking on a neighbor's door at midnight. Because of the man's persistence, the neighbor eventually gave him the loaves of bread he wanted. Here, persistence paid off for a desperate widow, who wanted a judgment against an adversary.

Jesus painted a picture of a judge who thought only of himself and was unjust in both his physical and spiritual existence. Because he respected no one, the widow's pleas to him fell on deaf ears for a long time. Yet, he caved in to the woman's pleas in the end, because he feared she would do him physical harm, and possible even sully his reputation with others in the town

(18:5). He also might have realized the woman was not seeking revenge, only justice for her case. It was Jesus' subtle way of telling his disciples that even the most wicked people can be turned into followers of God and the Good Way.

You might have noticed that this parable has a theme similar to the encounter in Matthew (15:21-28), in which the Canaanite woman approached Jesus, who seemingly ignored her fervent cries when she asked him to cure her daughter, who was possessed by a demon. Jesus told the woman he had come to save the lost children of Israel, and it was not right to throw food reserved for others and throw it to the dogs (15:24-26).

Now, we know the Lord was all-loving, so he was not being nasty or dismissive of the woman. Rather, he was testing her faith, and she did not disappoint him. In one of the most heartfelt statements of all in the gospels, she tearfully said, "Please, Lord, for even dogs eat the scraps that fall from the table of their masters" (15:27).

That woman had not only just passed the test Jesus had given her, but also astounded him, causing the Lord to say, "O woman, great is your faith! Let it be done for you as you wish" (15:28). Just as in the persistent neighbor and woman pleading with the judge, the Canaanite woman proved that pleading to God for grace and forgiveness will always have a wonderful and lasting result.

Dishonesty is not the Best Policy (Luke 16:1-8)

While we are on the subject of dishonesty and being unjust, we now look at a parable that demonstrates being so does not pay. A steward is the anti-hero in this story Jesus told to his disciples.

Being entrusted by a rich man for conducting the master's business affairs was a high honor for a servant. In some households, a rich man might not have even known what debtors had borrowed, because he left that to the servant who was his steward. The servant in this parable had a pretty good deal going for until his master got wind of some shady dealings the steward was pulling on the master's debtors. In short, he was adding to the debts, skimming a percentage off the top for himself. This, of course, was unethical and amoral (studylight.org).

All came crashing down for the steward when the rich man – probably learning of the steward's practices through the debtors themselves – hit the proverbial ceiling. We can only imagine the steward's reaction when, after being summoned by the master, found out his services were no longer required (16:2). Unlike the unforgiving servant from another parable, the rich man did not threaten his steward with prison; he just fired him. Back then, it would be a severe punishment in itself, for slaves had little standing in society and would have to scrape for a living if let go.

And that is exactly what this now-unemployed servant felt. He asked himself what he would do, now that he had no job. "I am not strong enough to dig, and I am ashamed to beg" (16:3). His status had indeed hit a nadir. But, devious people are also clever, so the steward, recovering from the shock of losing his job, felt there was a good chance one of those to whom he was lessening their debt would hire him because of his pretended largess (16:4).

Back to work he went, but for a renewed purpose. Calling each of his master's debtors in one by one, he reduced their debt considerably, making them happy. Of course, he was merely forfeiting his usurious percentage added to the debt but hoping none of the debtors would notice. We will never know if this clever scheme succeeded in his getting a new stewardship, but his master "commended' him for his resourcefulness (16:8).

We might ask ourselves why Jesus had the master praising this dishonest slave. He was really not doing so, for following the parable, the Lord told the disciples that one who is trustworthy in small matters is trustworthy in larger ones. Conversely, one who is not trustworthy with dishonest wealth is not so with honest wealth (16:10-12).

The point? If you are given the gift of faith and squander it through a life of sin, you are untrustworthy in that matter. However, if you lead a good life and use the gift God has given you for bettering yourself and others, then you are being trustworthy to your master, the living God. "You cannot serve God and mammon" (16:13).

Tax collector = Humble; Pharisee = Not so Much (Luke 18:9-14)

On a TV afternoon talk show some years ago, the hostess asked country singer Loretta Lynn if she thought she was above other people because of her talent and fame. It is unlikely the hostess was prepared for Lynn's brilliant response. She told the hostess, "I'm not better than anyone, and nobody's better than me." Wow!

How true was that memorable statement. We are all God's children, whether we have different skin colors, desires, ambitions, loves and hates, or whatever else. Every person on Earth belongs to our Creator. There are no exceptions.

Unfortunately, some people feel superior or inferior to others. We might envy those rich people in business, sports, or Hollywood and gawk at their lifestyle, but we also must keep in mind that this earthly life is fleeting, eternity is not. Keeping our eye on the ultimate prize will put everything else in perspective. That attitude was totally missing in the "star" in the parable of the Pharisee and the tax collector.

As we have learned in earlier parable discussions, tax collectors were considered far less than desirable, because – like the unjust steward – they often engaged in usurious practices, collecting money for themselves above and beyond that required by the Roman occupiers in Israel. Pharisees, as scholars of the law and spiritual leaders, also had their serious flaws, and Jesus was not at all hesitant to remind them of this. In Matthew (23:1-36) and Luke (11:39-54), the Lord gave stinging denunciations to the scribes, Pharisees and other scholars of the law for their superior attitude toward others, and for placing themselves on a pedestal so everyone could admire them. Loretta Lynn was eminently correct.

In the parable of the Pharisee and the tax collector, addressed to the twelve disciples, Jesus made it quite clear that the spiritual rules for the road include a very generous dose of humility. Placing ourselves over anyone else is not the way to spiritual success.

Was this not similar to the parable of Lazarus and the rich man? There, the rich man could not care less about Lazarus' plight. In this parable, there is a similar thread running through it. The Pharisee made it abundantly obvious that he considered himself superior to anyone else, especially the other man, who was in the back of the temple, too ashamed and humbled to approach the sanctuary. The contrast between the two men could not have been starker.

Even though the Pharisee said his words to himself and not aloud, God heard him just the same. Mister Self-Righteous thanked God not for being a man of faith, but rather for being above others. "O God, I thank you I am not like the rest of humanity – greedy, dishonest, adulterous – or even like this tax collector" (18:11). He went on to lecture God by noting he fasted twice a week and paid tithes. In effect he was saying, "Aren't I the most wonderful person ever created?"

While he thought grace after grace was filling his soul, the humble tax collector was far back, probably just inside the entrance, beating his breast and begging for God's mercy. "O God, be merciful to me, a sinner (18:13). Jesus then reminded his disciples that it was the tax collector who, in asking for God's mercy, went home justified, while the Pharisee was not so comforted.

It is not one's status in life that brings us true happiness; rather, it is being satisfied with what we have and thanking God for the gifts of life and faith. Again, Jesus told the disciples that those who exalt themselves will be humbled, but the humble of spirit will be exalted, for their faith is something they cherish to the depths of their soul.

The Fig Tree that "Spoke" Volumes (13:6-9)

The cursing of the fig tree in the gospels of Matthew and Mark is not a parable, but rather an event with the disciples as witnesses. It was, as we will now see, a lesson of the importance of not renouncing faith, but being unerringly strong. Luke does relate a parable involving a fig tree, and we will look at that, as well.

In the Old Testament, there are more than thirty references to figs and fig trees, most of which refer to the value of figs as food, or the good shade fig trees provide in warm weather as a shelter from the heat of the sun.

The first reference in the Bible to figs is Genesis 3:7, in which Adam and Eve sewed fig leaves together to clothe themselves. However, it is not true that one day Adam, being unable to find his loincloth said to Eve, "Honey, I think you just made the salad with my pants."

In the gospels, the fig tree played an important symbolic and cautionary role. Jesus, during the Sermon on the Mount, warned the assembled crowd that people do not pick figs from thistles. He emphasized that a good tree bears good fruit, while a bad tree bears rotten fruit, and all trees not bearing good fruit will be burned (Matthew 7:16-19; Luke 6:44).

That remark was to have a much more telling impact later, when Jesus cursed the fig tree for not having fruit, and it dried up immediately (Matthew 21:19). While Matthew did not provide more detail as to why Jesus cursed the fig tree, Mark (11:12-14) noted it was not the time for figs. Jesus, of course, knew this, yet he withered the tree, and his disciples heard him say this, though in Mark's version the tree did not immediately dry up. The next morning, Peter saw the fig tree had withered and pointed this out to Jesus. The Lord reminded Peter and the other disciples that faith can move mountains and implied that having an unshakable faith will never wither one's soul (Mark 11:22-25).

On the surface, cursing a tree with no fruit out of season might seem illogical, since Jesus, knowing everything, also knew before he even approached the tree that it would be barren of figs. That, however, was not the Lord's point. It was a lesson for the disciples to understand that they would be sent out later to spread the gospel far and wide, yet not all would listen. Like the fig tree, nonbelievers would shrivel up spiritually. Further, and more pointedly, it was a reference to the Nation Israel, which rejected his teaching and subsequently put him to death.

When the disciples saw the cursed fig tree had withered, Jesus simply told them, "Have faith in God…Therefore, I tell you, all that you ask for in prayer believe that you will receive it, and it shall be yours" (Mark 11:22; 24). Unlike the fig tree, they would prosper and help others prosper in faith, and they would not wither, but rather would bear good fruit.

In Luke's parable, a man looked in vain for three years for figs on a tree on his property. Frustrated, he ordered his gardener to cut it down, because it was producing nothing. The gardener, however, saw there might yet be hope for the tree bearing fruit and asked the owner to let him cultivate the soil around the tree. If nothing good happened, then the tree should be cut down (Luke 13:6-9).

God the Father was the homeowner in this parable, while Jesus was the gardener. The Son asked the father to let him give more chances to those people who did not bear the fruit of faith, because they might see the light of believing and come to God. If those who were "cultivated" over and over but who never bore fruit, then they could be condemned.

God never holds back forgiveness, even with those who reject him, until they die unrepentant and wither forever.

Wicked Tenants, Wretched End (Matthew 21:33-46)

It is appropriate to end our discussion of Jesus' parables with that of the wicket tenants, for this parable, told to the chief priests and elders, presents the most vivid and clear message of the consequences of sin and turning from God. It is one of only two parables – the other being the parable of the sower – to be written by all three synoptic gospel writers.

This parable has several symbolic meanings, all of which point to either the fate of Israel in the year 70 A.D., or the crucifixion and its consequences for those who rejected Jesus. It begins simply enough, with scarcely a hint of what will soon follow.

A landowner planted a vineyard, dug a wine press and then entrusted his vineyard to tenants he hired. He then went on a long journey, returning when vintage time was near, so naturally he expected to reap the reward of his efforts and those of the tenants.

Here, the vineyard represents the fertile field of the world's people, who are to be "harvested" for the eternal Kingdom. God the Father is the landowner who sends the prophets to preach repentance, but the tenants (the Nation of Israel) want nothing to do with the message. They beat and kill them and turn their back on God.

The landowner must have been almost in despair at the turn of events. He had fully expected the tenants to harvest the grapes, make wine and then be paid for all their good work. It seems strange that he let servants be beaten and killed without retaliating against them. Was he so naïve as to believe sending his son to that vineyard would have put fear into those wicked folks?

Well, God is not at all naïve; he is ever-loving. That is why he sent is Son into the vineyard (our world), because the tenants (Israel) would respect him. Of course, we know Jesus was not received by the tenants at all. They had him crucified, instead.

We also might wonder why the tenants were thinking that if they killed the landowner's son they would inherit the vineyard. At the time of Jesus, if a family's only son died, and there was no other heir, tenants on the land would have the final claim to it (New American Bible in Matthew, Chapter 21, footnote). Yes, but the tenants in this parable were criminals and murderers, which would have precluded any claim they might file for the vineyard.

That is why Jesus had warned, over and over, that the Jews, for whom he had come, would not inherit the Kingdom because of their unbelief. Rather, the Faith would go to others who embraced the gospel and his words: "Did you never read in the scriptures: 'The stone that the builders rejected has become the cornerstone; by the Lord has this been done, and is wonderful in our eyes'" ? (Psalm 118:22-23).

In a further warning to those listening that day, he added, "Therefore, I say to you that the kingdom of God will be taken away from you and be given to a people that will produce its fruit" (21:42-43). Rather than heed Jesus and his plea to them, the chief priests and Pharisees sought to arrest him, but they did not, for others hearing the message saw Jesus as a prophet (21:46).

Recall the earlier parable we discussed, that of the wedding feast (Matthew (22:1-13), which had a very similar message and warning. It also depicted servants being beaten and killed, with an enraged king burning the cities of those perpetrators. Again, those who had been invited to the eternal kingdom were not to be admitted. The servants (disciples) were to gather others to enjoy the never-ending banquet.

The wonderful gift of Faith from God is something to be cherished every minute of every day. Heaven awaits!

Section XII – The Immortal Metaphors in John's Gospel

John's gospel is entirely different from the synoptic gospels of Matthew, Mark and Luke in its approach. There are no parables to be found in its twenty-one chapters, but rather it contains a more theological approach to the Savior's messages to his audiences, disciples and individuals. To be sure, there are miracles, cures and warnings, just as there re in the synoptic writings, but the fourth gospel is oriented to the theological mission for which Jesus was sent to Earth, not to a summary of his life and activities.

Throughout this section, all chapter and verse notifications are from John's gospel, unless otherwise stated. The Fourth Gospel shows a different way in which Jesus prefaced his statements referring to himself. He employed the metaphorical usage with the powerful expression of "I am, or even more emphatrically, I AM.." Compare that with his prefacing so many of his parables in the synoptic gospels, where he introduced many parables, saying, "The kingdom of heaven is like…"

John makes Jesus' claim to be the Son of God abundantly clear by showing the Lord did not couch his Sonship in vague terms, but instead boldly proclaimed it in those two definitive words, "I am." As we are about to see, Jesus echoed his Father six times to hammer home in even more emphatic way the point he was the immortal Son, on the second word.

There is an Old Testament precedent to "I AM". In Exodus (3:14), God replied very pointedly to Moses, when the latter asked what he should say to the Israelites if they asked God's name: "I am who am. He then added, "This what you should tell the Israelites: I AM sent me."

The infinite Father's no-nonsense reply told Moses that there was to be no doubt or argument.

Fast-forward some centuries and we find John showing Jesus making the same emphatic statement to the Pharisees. After Jesus had forgiven the woman about to be stoned for adultery (8:1-11), he lectured the Pharisees on the importance of believing in him for embracing things of the world, not of heaven" "If you do not believe that I AM, you will die in your sins" (8:24).

The Lord emphasized his divinity twice more in John 8. The second time was in regard to the crucifixion to which he would be condemned, perhaps by the same Pharisees he was addressing, saying, "When you lift up the Son of Man, then you will realize that I AM, and that I do nothing on my own, but I say only what the Father taught me" (8:28). The third such statement is in John 8:58. There, Jesus told the Pharisees he existed prior to human beings, after he told the Pharisees he pre-dated Abraham: "Amen, amen, I say to you, before Abraham came to be, I AM".

Now, either Jesus was guilty of bad grammatical usage, or he was asserting his Divine nature. We know, of course, that he was showing the unbelieving Jewish leaders he was from the Father, not of earthly origin. This infuriated the Pharisees, because they saw him as "blaspheming" and tried to stone him to death on the spot. Since his hour for suffering had not yet come, the Lord hid himself and left the temple area (8:58-59).

We will see several more "I AM" statements in John's gospel in the context of Jesus stating his divinity, but for now let us examine many other "I am" (no capital letters for "am") and other references from Jesus as he preached salvation to the Jews.

The Eternal Word

John's magnificent prologue begins by naming Jesus "the Word" (1:1) and goes on to name him "the light" that shone on the darkness, which the darkness could not shut down (1:5). The preaching of John the Baptist gave testimony to the light which had come into the world to enlighten every human being (1:9). And then we have that wonderful, inspired statement, "And the Word became flesh and made his dwelling among us, and we saw his glory…" (1:14). It was no coincidence that Jesus was later to refer to himself as "the light of the world. Whoever follows me will not walk in darkness, but will have the light of life" (8:12).

Before we get too far ahead of ourselves, let us back up to the entrance of Jesus into his ministry. Just as a modern-day emcee happily introduces the main speaker at an important event, John the Baptist saw Jesus coming toward him as he was baptizing and cried out, "Behold the Lamb of God, who takes away the sins of the world" (1:29). He repeated that exhortation the next day, as two of his own disciples were present. They immediately left John to follow Jesus (1:36-37).

A somewhat amusing occurrence happened the next day, when Jesus added Philip to his yet-small knot of disciples. Philip, overjoyed at being called to discipleship, ran to a friend and possibly mentor, Nathanael, proclaiming excitedly Jesus was the one about whom Moses wrote. Unconvinced, Nathanael said sarcastically, "Can anything good come from Nazareth?" (1:44-46). That little town did not produce great leaders and was considered less than valuable by Jews. Yet, Nathanael, stunned by the way Jesus then spoke to him, said "Rabbi, you are the Son of God!" (1:49). In effect, Nathanael was the first convert other than a disciple, to what was to become Christianity.

Cana – The First Miracle

"They have no wine" (2:3). So said Mary, the mother of Jesus, to her Son as they enjoyed a wedding feast. In ancient Israel, running out of wine – an important part of a wedding event – would have brought lasting shame upon the bride and groom and their families. An enigmatic, though brief, sequence followed. Jesus apparently brushed off his mother's statement dismissively. He said, "Woman, how does your concern affect me? My hour has not yet come" (2:4).

The word, "woman," was actually a sign of respect in those days. It might have given Mary the assurance she needed that Jesus would accede to her asking for his help. Indeed, Mary knew Jesus was not brushing her off and she immediately told the servers to do whatever he wanted. His first miracle followed, and the day for the families was saved. Not only did Jesus turn water into wine, he made the best wine for that feast.

Despite his initial question to his mother. Was he just testing Mary, or was he annoyed that she should have had the nerve to ask for a favor? Mary knew, in her heart, that Jesus would do as she wished. The turning of water into wine was thus a metaphor for the new Faith, the water of faith practices were to become the wine of pure substance, instituted at the Last Supper. The miracle at Cana was a prelude to the Last Supper and institution of the Eucharist.

Destroy This Temple..."

In Christian belief, the human body is the temple of the Holy Spirit, the Paraclete, who guides us in faith and good works throughout our life. Jesus referred to his own body in that way after he angrily drove the money-changers and sellers of sheep and cattle from the temple of worship. The Jews then demanded a sign for Jesus to authenticate why he was committing such an act. Jesus' seemingly oblique answer was, "Destroy this temple and in three days I will raise it up" (2:19). The Jews thought he was referring to the temple where they worshipped, but he meant his body, which would rise from the grave three days after his crucifixion. He said that not so much for the Jews' benefit, but for the disciples to understand, as they did after his Resurrection (2:22).

Death can and will destroy our bodies, but our souls will rise from the grave. At the end of all time, our bodies will once again be reunited and we will be whole forever in the Kingdom.

Born Again, Forever

Reading the account of Nicodemus visiting Jesus (3:1-21), we can see a bit of humor, mixed with frustration, on the part of the Lord. Nicodemus, a ruler of the Jews, came surreptitiously at night to see Jesus. He might well have been looking over his shoulder, not wanting the Pharisees or other Jewish leaders to know about his visit, since they were already hostile to Jesus.

He admitted to Jesus that he saw him as being from God and thus was a believer in the Lord. However, this well-intentioned leader was floored when Jesus said, "...no one can see the kingdom of God without being born from above" (3:3). Poor Nicodemus, who could not fathom what that meant and wondered how someone could re-enter his mother's womb and be born again (3:4).

Jesus might well have rolled his eyes at that one, but even his subsequent explanation of what he meant went right over the head of Nicodemus, who then asked, "How can this happen?" (3:9). The sigh from the Lord must have been palpable as he said, a bit exasperated, "You are a teacher of Israel and you do not understand this?" (3:10). He then revealed he was from heaven and would be killed, so all would believe in him as the Son of God and would be saved through this belief (3:11-15). Jesus emphasized he was the light of the world, and those who live the truth of his teaching will come to the light – himself (3:20-21).

There is no question that what Jesus spoke to Nicodemus metaphorically that night had a life-changing impact on that Jewish leader. After the crucifixion and death of Jesus, he was at the cross with Joseph of Arimathea to help anoint and bury Jesus' body in the tomb (20:38-39). Faith lesson learned well.

Hope for Samaritans

Another touch of humor, coupled with (as always) a lesson for the disciples, is found when a Samaritan woman and Jesus met at Jacob's well. As noted earlier in this work, Jews had nothing to do with Samaritans, whom the considered ritually impure, especially Samaritan women (4:9). They would, however, venture into a Samaritan town for food if on a journey. That was the case when Jesus rested near the town of Sychar at the well, while his disciples went into the town for food.

Along came a Samaritan woman, and Jesus shocked her by asking her to give him a drink of water (4:7). It was highly unusual for a man to speak with a woman one-on-one, especially a Samaritan, let alone ask for a drink. Undeterred by that and by the woman's response, after she told Jesus she was a Samaritan and he was a Jew, Jesus let the woman know he was living water "that I shall give will become in him a spring of water welling up to eternal life" (4:14).

Of course, the woman did not understand the meaning of the Lord's words and thought he would cure her physical thirst forever and save her from more trips to the well. After all, the water bucket was heavy when filled, and she would be relieved of a tedious duty.

At that point, a bit of wry humor on the Lord's part came to pass. Jesus told the woman to come back with her husband. Sheepishly, the woman admitted she had no husband, and Jesus noted she was correct. "You are right in saying 'I do not have a husband,' for you have had five husbands, and the one you have now is not your husband" (4:16-18). Ouch!

Jesus then proclaimed his Messiahship to the woman, who went back to Sychar and rounded up the entire town to go and see the Messiah. Jesus stayed in that town for two days and many came to believe in him, thanks to a sinful woman who helped bring a whole town into faith.

This episode also provided Jesus with a critical lesson for his disciples. Not only did he accept water from a Samaritan and a woman (contrary to Jewish law), but he also emphasized salvation for all by this example. Further, he hinted that he would provide an eternal food to eat "of which you do not know" (4:32). This cryptic metaphor would become crystal clear to the disciples at the Last Supper, when Jesus instituted the Eucharist – the food which would never leave anyone spiritually hungry.

Spiritual Thirst Slaked

In Jerusalem for the Passover feast, Jesus spoke to the assembled throng in the temple, saying, "Let anyone who thirsts come to me and drink" (7:37-38). Once again, the crowd was divided, with some praising Jesus as a prophet and others asking how he could say such things.

Nicodemus, now a believer, tried to assuage the priests and Pharisees, who had sent guards to arrest Jesus. He urged the other Jewish leaders to first hear Jesus before condemning him. The other leaders, always ready to get rid of Jesus forever, reminded Nicodemus that no prophet ever came from Galilee (7:51-52). Their minds were made up as to what they wanted to do with Jesus, and no one was to stand in their way.

Five Barley Loaves? "Barley" Enough? Not Really! (Matthew 14:13-21; Mark 8:1-9; Luke 9:10-17; John 6:1-13)

Yet another of Jesus' lessons to the disciples involving bread and its eternal quality occurred in the feeding of thousands of people as they listened to him. The disciples wondered how they could feed such a throng, but when Peter's brother Andrew noted a boy at the scene had five barley loaves and two fish, all were fed.

When he told the people that the Father gives bread from heaven to give life to the world, the people wanted to have that bread always. So, Jesus once again said it was he who *was* what they sought: "I am the bread of life; whoever comes to me will never hunger, and whoever believes in me will never thirst" (6:34-35). This led the Jews to wonder what he meant, questioning, "How can this man give us is flesh to eat?" (6:52).

All four gospels recount the feeding of a huge crowd, but only in John's gospel is the type of bread stated. Andrew, Peter's brother, told Jesus a boy in the crowd had five barley loaves and two fish (John 6:9). In Matthew (14:17), Mark (8:5), and Luke (9:13), there is no mention of a boy with bread and fish. Matthew and Luke mention five loaves and two fish, while Mark says there were seven loaves, but no mention of fish.

What is the significance of the type of bread? In ancient Israel, wheat produced a better-quality bread. Barley bread was coarser and smaller by the loaf, as well as being unleavened. It was a staple for poor people who could not afford the cost of wheat to make their bread (from "Hidden Symbols in the Loaves and Fish", online at torahportions.ff02.org). Jesus was making the point that even the poorest were to be fed the Bread of eternal life.

Food Eternally Better Than Bread

In his discourse on the Bread of Life (6:22-59), the Lord promised an eternal bread, which those hearing him asked Jesus to give it to them. Others wondered, with great disbelief, how Jesus could be the bread that came down from heaven. After all, he was human and the son of Mary and Joseph. How could he promise such a thing? The Jews were even more confused when Jesus added, "I am the living bread that cane down from heaven; whoever eats this bread will live forever, and the bread I will give is my flesh for the life of the world" (6:51).

Not deterred by the murmuring among the Jews after they heard that promise, Jesus added. "Whoever eats my flesh and drinks my blood has eternal life, and I will raise him up on the last day" (6:54).

Admittedly, it must have been a strange concept for the Jews or anyone else present that day. Let us be honest: If we heard someone say we could eat his flesh and drink his blood, would we believe him?

Remember, the Jews did not expect a man of humble origins to be a mighty prophet. Many who had become disciples said among themselves, "This saying is hard; who can accept it?" (6:60). As a result, many turned from Jesus for good. Little wonder Jesus asked the Twelve if they, too, wanted to leave him. But Peter, always the faithful one, gave a beautiful and touching answer: "Master, to whom shall we go? You have the words of eternal life. We have come to believe and are convinced that you are the holy one of God" (6:68-69).

Despite Peter's staunch remark of faith, Jesus did not praise that disciple, or any of the others. Instead, he reminded them that one among them was a devil. Even knowing most were to stand by him, the Lord felt the bitterness knowing that one of those trusted men would help condemn him to a horrible death.

A Light That Burns Eternally

When the scribes and Pharisees dragged a woman caught in adultery to Jesus, little did they know he would send them packing in shame with just a few well-chosen words: "Let the one among you who is without sin be the first to throw a stone at her" (8:7). He then showed those leaders true charity by forgiving the woman's sins.

That was not the end of the session. Jesus spoke again to those leaders, calling himself the light of the world (8:12). Naturally, the scribes and Pharisees took strong exception to that claim, accusing Jesus of speaking on his own behalf. Then, the Lord gave those leaders another strong lesson in his being the Son of God, including his eternal nature by proclaiming "I AM" (8:24; 8:58). Things did not go well for Jesus at that encounter. The scribes and Pharisees accused Jesus of being a Samaritan and also being possessed (8:48). They even tried to stone him but did not succeed (8:59). The Light (Jesus) did not flicker at all, but that of the Jewish leaders never flared into existence.

The Blind See; the Sighted Do Not

John (9:1-5) again noted that Jesus called himself the light of the world and at the same time proclaimed metaphorically that the blind see but those with sight do not. He cured a blind man with his disciples as witnesses, saying, "While I am in the world, I am the light of the world" (9:5).

There is another metaphor in that statement. After smearing clay on the blind man's eyes, Jesus told him to wash in the Pool of Siloam (9:7). Washing is symbolic of cleansing, so the blind man gained sight and also, in effect, was baptized by the pool's water.

Now, this should have opened the Pharisees eyes, figuratively, to what Jesus was accomplishing, but that did not happen. Their minds remained closed, even as the blind man worshipped Jesus and expressed his belief in him (9:38-39). The Lord then told the formerly blind man that the blind see, but those who see are blind (9:39). Again, the Pharisees took exception, claiming they were not blind, but Jesus was not buying any of it. "If you were blind, you would have no sin; but now you are saying, 'We see,' so your sin remains" (9:41). Blindness is not just eyesight, but also can be a denial of the truth.

John (9:1-41), contains the longest of all the gospel references to men who were blind. After telling the disciples he was the light of the world while on Earth, he cured a young man of his blindness. This led to not only disbelief by the Jewish leaders and others, but also to an interrogation of the young man's parents. In the end, the angry, disbelieving Pharisees threw the cured man out of their meeting place. Jesus found the young man and asked him if he believed in the Son of Man. The young man said he did and worshipped Jesus (9:35-38).

Jesus then said to the Pharisees, "I came into this world for judgment, so that those who do not see might see, and those who do see might become blind" (9:39). Those who did not accept his teaching might see physically, but were totally blind to the truth.

Other blind men Jesus cured, noted in the three synoptic gospels, pleaded with him earnestly: "Jesus, Son of David, have pity on us (or me)!" (Matthew 9:27 and 20:30; Mark 10:47; Luke 18:38). Metaphorically, those blind men "saw" Jesus as the Messiah and knew he could make them see. The Lord never did anything without a good reason. In curing blindness in those who had spiritual sight, he showed the disciples and the Jewish leaders that being able to see both spiritually and physically was the key to eternal life. Jesus demonstrated that in life the blind see the right path, while others do no because of their hardened hearts.

The Good Shepherd

In the parables section of this work, we saw the gentleness of sheep and the loyalty of the shepherd to them. John's gospel contains the poignant account of Jesus trying to show his gentle leadership to the Jewish leaders by calling himself the good shepherd and the gate for the sheep (10:7; 11). Again, this is the kind of imagery to which his listeners could relate and was also a statement hinting at his upcoming Passion and death. Further, this is yet another example of the Lord predicting his own death: "I am the good shepherd. A good shepherd lays down his life for the sheep" (10:11). As could have been predicted, the Jews were conflicted as to what Jesus meant. Some thought he was possessed; others considered him a prophet, not a devil (10:21).

Three times, Jesus called himself the good shepherd in that message to the Jewish leaders. He seamlessly interwove not only his gentle nature with the metaphor of sheep and shepherd, but also boldly talked about his death and his being the Son of God, saying, "I and the Father are one" (10:7-30. This enraged the Jews to the point that they tried to stone him for blasphemy, but Jesus continued by stating "the Father is in me and I am in the Father" (10:38). The Lord then evaded their effort to arrest him on the spot. He escaped and went across the Jordan River, where many came to believe in him (10:40-42).

One Resurrection Leading to Another

Jesus' greatest miracle was raising Lazarus from the dead (11:1-44). In doing so, he demonstrated to one and all that death has no power over anyone. All who believe will be raised to live forever.

Before raising Lazarus, however, Jesus did not even hurry to Bethany where Lazarus and his sisters, Mary and Martha, lived. Rather, he stayed away for two days. It was to be another important lesson for his disciples, and in no way was a deliberate act of not caring. Jesus was simply laying the groundwork for the incredible miracle of bringing Lazarus back to life and previewing his own death and resurrection.

This continued when he encountered Martha as he came to Bethany. After telling Jesus her brother would not have died had he been there sooner, Martha further expressed her strong faith in him, saying she knew Lazarus would rise again at the end of time (11:24). It was then Jesus said to her, "I am the resurrection and the life; whoever believes in me, even if he dies, will live, and everyone who lives and believes in me will never die" (11:25-26). Martha, she of incredible faith in Jesus, said to him, "Yes, Lord. I have come to believe that you are the Messiah, the Son of God..." (11:27).

Moments later, Mary, Martha's sister, said much the same thing about her brother's being alive had Jesus come sooner. Jesus became deeply engrossed in sorrow and wept. Why? He might well have been looking into the future. Even after witnessing the stunning bringing back a life from the dead, the Sanhedrin still wanted to kill Jesus, because they feared the occupying Romans would take away their land after Jesus brought all to his way of life (11:48). So, it is reasonable to say Jesus knew that even bringing a dead man back to life would not be enough to bring many to believe.

In raising the Lazarus in John's gospel, Jesus was making the strongest point possible that life is not unending. Alas, that was lost on the Jewish leaders, so the tears Jesus shed that day were those of extreme sorrow over people's lack of belief. He knew raising Lazarus would only incense the Sanhedrin and other leaders to the boiling point. And, he also knew his hour of extreme suffering was nigh. Little wonder he showed such grief to those at the tomb. Not all believed he was, indeed, the Resurrection and the Life. Nor do they, to this day.

An Ass, Not a Steed

"Take my yoke upon you and learn from me, for I am gentle and humble in heart, and you will find rest for your souls" (Matthew11:29).

Jesus showed his humble nature when he rode an ass into Jerusalem to the cheering of the crowd (John 12:12-15). No princely Arab horse for the Lord, just a simple animal that underscored his message that he was for all the people, regardless of stature in life. It is difficult to comprehend that this triumphant entry, with the masses spreading palm branches to honor him, would suddenly become his Passion. It was no coincidence that the Pharisees observed the triumphant entry and told each other, "Look, the whole world has gone after him" (12:19). The plot against Jesus had begun to thicken.

Jesus already knew this, and he told his disciples he was troubled, but his hour had come and, following his torture and death would bring all people to himself (12:32). He then told the crowd that he, the light, was to be taken from them, but he urged everyone to believe in the light, "so you may become children of the light:" (12:36). And then, he urged the crowd to understand he was speaking what the Father told him what to say. Those who rejected him would be condemned by the Father on the last day for not accepting the Son (12:47-50).

Washing Feet: An Act of Humility

Perhaps it is difficult to grasp behind the meaning of Jesus washing the feet of his disciples. It was, however, another great act of humility by the Son of God. Further, it was a symbolic lesson for the Twelve, for they were to do what he had just done (13:15). As he had served them by performing this seemingly demeaning gesture, so were the disciples to cleanse sins from those whose lives they touched by baptizing them with water. They were to be the messengers of the faith Jesus was establishing. but had also to remember they were no greater than Jesus, who was sending them to spread the gospel (13:16). Hence, the deeper meaning of his washing the disciples' feet.

A pall of silence surely fell on the group after the foot-washing, when Jesus cautioned his friends "when it (his crucifixion and death) happens, you may believe that I AM" (13:19). Yet, they most likely did not understand what Jesus meant when he told the now-Eleven (Judas had left on his mission of betrayal), when he said they would not go where he was about to go (13:33). Peter, ever the outspoken one, asked Jesus point blank, "Where are you going?" (13:36). He then told the Lord he would die for him, and Jesus rebuked him by saying he would deny the Master three times before the cock crowed (13:37-38). We can only speculate on how Peter reacted to the Lord's prediction, but as we will see later in this section, the three-time denial Jesus predicted was to result in a three-time forgiveness after the Resurrection. All missteps in life, including even the most serious sins, can be forgiven.

I am the Way...

Peter was not alone in asking Jesus where he was going. Thomas, at the Last Supper, also asked the same question" Master, we do not know where you are going; how can we know the way?" (14:5). The Lord's answer was gentle and unequivocal: "I am the way the truth and the life. No one comes to the Father except through me" (14:6).

It does not get any plainer or more emphatic than that. Notice Jesus did not say, "I show you the way," but rather, "I *am* the way the truth and the life." The Lord was reminding the disciples of his divinity as the Son of God.

Some might question the second part of Jesus' statement, "No one comes to the Father except through me." Was he excluding non-Christians or others who believe in God but do not worship Jesus? Not at all! By accepting God as their Father, all believers, regardless of faith, belong not only to Him, but also to the Son and the Holy Spirit. All of us are God's children; all of us have the same path to eternal life.

"I am the Vine"

During the Last Supper discourses in John's gospel, Jesus provided messages and lessons that were both encouraging and cautionary. It was his final opportunity to lay the groundwork for the disciples before his arrest and subsequent Passion and death. Just as he called himself the way the truth and the life, the Lord also called himself the true vine, and those who remained in him would bear much fruit (15:5).

Preceding and following that statement of great hope to his disciples, Jesus added a stern warning. First, the Father discards every branch that does not bear fruit (those who do not believe in or worship God), and those who do not accept Jesus also will be cast out and burned in the fire (15:2; 6).

Softening that statement of eternal punishment, Jesus assured the remaining eleven disciples that because they believed in him he loved them as much as the Father loved him. "Remain in my love, just as I have kept my Father's commandments and remain in his love" (15:10). And then, "This is my commandment: Love one another as I have loved you. No one has greater love than this, to lay down one's life for one's friends" (15:12-13). Once again, Jesus was pointing to his imminent Passion, but also letting the disciples know they would never be without him.

The Arrest of "I AM"

Earlier in this section, we discussed Jesus' apparently unusual use of "I AM", to let others know he was the eternal Son of God. So, when Judas arrived with a mob of soldiers and guards armed with torches and weapons, Jesus posed a rhetorical question: "Whom are you looking for?" (18: 4).He admitted who he was but with the emphatic "I AM", (18:6; 8).

Such an admission had no effect on those sent to arrest him, for they did not accept his claim to be God's Son. Also, those arresting him might well have just taken the Lord's words as simply admitting his identity. They had no idea whatever that this "criminal" was divine and the Son of God. Their job was to find Jesus and bring him to the Jewish authorities, nothing more.

Thus, they bound him and carted him off to the Jewish officials. The greatest travesty in human history had just begun.

Peter's Metaphorical Denials

All four gospels depict Peter as one of the most astute of the twelve disciples. It was he who confessed to Jesus being the Son of God (Matthew 16:16; Mark 8:29, Luke 9:20) and was also chosen, along with James and John, to witness the transfiguration. His belief in Jesus was unwavering, even to his proclaiming to Jesus that he would die for him. The Lord had to negate that bold statement by letting Peter know he would deny even knowing him after his arrest (Matthew 26: 33-35; Mark 14: 29-31; Luke 22: 33-34); John 13: 37-38).

Peter must have been shaken to his core by that response, yet not knowing, what tragedy lay ahead. After the arrest of Jesus, Peter followed discreetly into the courtyard of the high priest (John 18:16). Because the evening was cool, the disciple stood by a charcoal fire, warming himself. Along came a maid, who asked Peter if he was one of Jesus' disciples. Peter denied even knowing Jesus.

Then, others asked him if he was a disciple, and Peter denied it again. Finally came the third denial, when a slave of the high priest who had been in the arresting crowd asked, "Didn't I see you in the garden with him?" (18:26-27). Then, the cock crowed and Peter, realizing his great act of disavowing he even knew Jesus, left the courtyard and wept bitterly (Matthew 26:75).

It would be easy to ask why Peter was not banished from discipleship after denying he even knew Jesus. After all, did Judas not offer a similar denial when he betrayed the Lord? After Peter's third denial, Jesus turned and looked at the disciple (Luke 23:61). That stare reduced Peter to bitter tears, but it also paved the way for a restoration to Jesus' good graces.

Peter's Metaphorical Restoration to Grace

There was much uncertainty among the followers of Jesus after the Resurrection, even though he had appeared to the Twelve, Mary Magdalene and others. The Holy Spirit had not yet blessed their mission to all people, and the disciples were likely becoming restless, wondering what was coming next. Peter, especially, was probably wishing for Jesus' special blessing to atone him for what happened in the high priest's courtyard. He did not have long to wait.

It occurred at the Sea of Tiberias when Peter announced he was going fishing. He and seven other disciples climbed into a boat and caught nothing. At dawn, they saw Jesus (disguised) on the shore, and he told those in the boat to cast their nets. The haul was one hundred fifty-three large fish, a symbolic number in itself, since that was the number of fish species known at that time (footnote in the New American Bible, John 21:11). It was John who cried, "It is the Lord", after the disciples pulled in that large number of fish (21:7). And then Peter tore off his outer garment in excitement and swam to shore.

Jesus provided fish for their breakfast, and then took Peter aside and asked him three times, "Peter, son of John, do you love me more than these"? Peter affirmed his love of Jesus, who then told the disciple his mission was to spread the gospel by feeding the sheep (21:15-17). The three denials in the courtyard had been wiped away; the three-time act of forgiveness restored Peter to grace once and for all.

Looking beneath the restoration of Peter to grace is an even stronger message for all of humanity. Yes, Peter's denial of Jesus stemmed from fear and uncertainty. But what Jesus' forgiveness on the shore of the Sea of Tiberias carried a much deeper meaning for all. No matter how great our sin, no matter how far we fall from grace, God's forgiveness is always thereif we sincerely ask for forgiveness. Jesus is there at all times and in every way for all of us.

Later Jesus' forgiveness of Peter turned into something even greater. On Pentecost, Peter and the other disciples were all gathered together, and the Holy Spirit came upon them like a strong wind with tongues of fire that settled on their heads (Acts 2: 3-4). They were now ready to preach Jesus to the entire world, and they did so, admirably and with the greatest zeal. The New Way had begun.

Subtle Metaphors in John's Gospel

In addition to the metaphors Jesus spoke regarding his Sonship, there are others in the Fourth Gospel, as well as in the synoptic gospels. We will focus on John's gospel for purposes of this part of our journey.

Significance of the Jordan River

Following the death of Moses, God appointed his aide, Joshua, to lead the Israelites into the Promised Land. To attain that goal, all Israelites had to cross the Jordan River. Just as God had dried up the Red Sea when the Israelites were escaping from Egypt, so did He dry up the Jordan so the nation could claim their land at last. The crossing began with the priests carrying the Ark of the Covenant, but they themselves did not enter the new land until all the people had preceded them over the now-dried river (Joshua 3:17). God then instructed Joshua to take twelve stones, each representing one of the twelve Tribes, and place them as a memorial (4:1-7).

Centuries later, John the Baptist was baptizing across that same river (Matthew 3:6; Mark 1:5; Luke 3:7; John1:31). Jesus approached him and John cried out, "Behold the Lamb of God, who takes away the sin of the world" (John 1:29).

That day, Jesus was baptized and entered into his sacred ministry of redemption. Hundreds of years earlier, the Israelites had crossed the Jordan River to enter the Promised Land. By no coincidence, Jesus crossed the Jordan to bring the promise of eternal life to that same nation and beyond, to the ends of the earth. The New Way for all of humanity and the new Promised Land of heaven began at that symbolic river.

The first Convert to Jesus?

Earlier, we learned the reason for Jesus' cursing of the unproductive fig tree. In John (1:45-51), we see the immediate confession of faith by Nathanael, a Jewish scholar of the Law. As we saw earlier, Nathanael was a bit of a cynic. Philp told Nathanael that Jesus was from Nazareth and the doubting scholar said, probably sarcastically, "Can anything good come from Nazareth?" (1:45-46). Such doubt did not last long, for Nathanael was stunned by the fact Jesus had seen him under a fig tree, even before he met him. Without a second's pause, Nathanael said to Jesus, "Rabbi, you are the Son of God; you are the king of Israel!" (1:49).

The symbolism here is that the fig tree was considered a place of peace for spiritual reflection. The prophet Micah wrote: "Every man shall sit…under his own fig tree, undisturbed…" (4:4). And the prophet Zechariah, recalling the day God made Joshua the high priest and promised removal Israel's sin guilt, said: "On that day, says the Lord of hosts, you will invite one another under your vines and fig trees" (3:9-10).

Thus, the fig tree also had a Messianic meaning, which bore spiritual fruit for Nathanael. He became a believer on the spot.

The First Woman Convert?

Following her encounter with Jesus, the Samaritan woman at Jacob's well (4:4-41), like Nathanael, became a believer in him. The Lord shocked her by revealing all he knew about her five marriages and her then-live-in boyfriend. It was also to that woman Jesus imparted knowledge to her about his being living water, then telling her he was the Messiah (4:26).

That woman instantly heralded to the town of Sychar everything Jesus had revealed, and the entire town suddenly recognized that there was a Jew in whom they could have faith. So, in addition to being convinced Jesus was the Messiah, the woman also became a *de facto* disciple to her people. Jesus was the Messiah for all.

Samaritans 'R Us, Too

Samaritans, as we noted elsewhere in this work, were despised by Israeli Jews because they had intermarried with non-Jewish people and had set up their own temple. Indeed, even Jesus cautioned the twelve disciples as he sent them out to preach the Good News not to enter any Samaritan town (Matthew 10:5). This was not a condemnation of Samaritans, but rather a limitation Jesus placed on the disciples for their first preaching mission. The Lord's specific instruction was, "Go rather to the lost sheep of the house of Israel" (10:6).

Though Jesus had an up-and-down relationship with people living in Samaritan villages, he had no such problem using individual Samaritans as examples of people doing good or being grateful to Him. He was rejected by Samaritans as he prepared to travel to Jerusalem and accept his Passion and death. That village refused to welcome him because Jerusalem was his destination (Luke 10: 52). Prejudice by both Israelites and Samaritans was mutual.

Conversely, Jesus brought Samaritans into a far better light by using them as examples and lessons to the Jews in the Good Samaritan parable, in a cured leper, and in the woman at Jacob's well. Why? To show the disciples and those who doubted his being the Messiah that salvation was for all, not just the Jewish people. Further, it was those Samaritans who were more faithful and deeply grateful for what Jesus did for them.

The Good Samaritan was the most outstanding example of the need to practice charity to others and do good works. The cleansed leper, also a Samaritan, was also the only one of the ten Jesus cured who not only returned to praise God, but to fall prostrate in gratitude (Luke 17:11-19). It was yet another pointed lesson Jesus used in the presence of those with him. The Samaritan was eternally grateful and was not hesitant to return and pay homage to Jesus. The other nine simply took their cure for granted. Were they Jews? We will never know, but we do know their gratitude was very limited.

Jesus also had to endure a stinging rebuke by the Jews as they rejected what they considered his radical teaching. Even as he preached to the Jews that he was sent by the Father and was speaking the truth t them about who he was, the Jews thought he was a charlatan and said, "Are we not right in saying that you are a Samaritan and are possessed?" (John 8:48).

Calling Jesus a Samaritan was a grave insult, as well as a rejection. Yet, he simply continued his claim to Sonship with the Father, which ended up in the crowd trying to stone him (8:59). As Jesus said, "A prophet is not without honor except in his native place and among his own kin and in his own house" (Matthew 13: 57; Mark 6: 4). He served everyone, including the Samaritans, who were just a worthy as any others.

Remaking the Sabbath

Imagine needing medical help on a Sunday – the traditional Sabbath day for most Christians – and being told, "Sorry, but we cannot help on the Sabbath. Call tomorrow." Ridiculous? Of course, but in ancient Israel, curing or doing anything else considered unlawful on the Sabbath was strictly forbidden. That changed with Jesus, who turned the prohibition on its head and sent a message that God works every day; therefore, the Sabbath was to be no exception.

"For the Son of Man is Lord of the Sabbath" (Matthew 12:8; Mark 2:28; Luke 6:1). Pretty heady claim, for sure, but then again Jesus had a very good reason for calling himself that. Because the Pharisees took strong exception to him when he cured people in need a number of times on the Sabbath, the Lord made it very clear he had every right to do so.

Prior to claiming his position as the Son of Man, the Pharisees complained that the disciples were violating the Sabbath by picking heads of grain and eating them (Matthew 12:2; Mark 2:23). Jesus had to remind those Jewish leaders that David and his companions ate the temple bread which only the temple priests were allowed to eat, when they were very hungry (1 Samuel 21:2-7).

Jesus scandalized the Pharisees still further after doing good deeds on the Sabbath. He immediately entered the temple and, as the Pharisees watched, cured the man with a withered hand (Mark 3:1-6). Filled with hatred, those Jewish leaders went out and discussed how to put this interloper to death (Matthew 12:14; Mark 3: 6). 14).

Other cures on the Sabbath included the woman who was bent over for eighteen years (Luke 13:11-17), the man with dropsy (inordinate swelling of the body) (Luke 14:2-5), and the man who was crippled for thirty-eight years (John 5:3-9). Each cure was either witnessed by the Pharisees or discovered – in the case of the cured crippled man carrying his mat – that Jesus had yet defied the Sabbath by effecting cures.

Even though the Lord chastised the Pharisees and said he was doing the Father's work any day, including the Sabbath, those obstinate leaders continued to look for a way to put him to death. No matter how many times Jesus proclaimed his mission to the Jewish leaders, their hearts became even more hardened against him Sabbath. It was a no-win situation for him with the Pharisees and others in Israel.

Forgiveness is Always There, Even at the Point of Death

Peter denied he even knew Jesus, when confronted three times in the courtyard of the high priest. Because God is all-forgiving, Jesus restored him to full grace following his resurrection.

That alone tells us that forgiveness for our sins is never-ending. Yet, there is an even more dramatic example of a grievous sinner saved from eternal damnation, and it is perhaps the most wonderful of all Jesus' forgiveness actions. This episode was not in John, but rather in Luke.

Two wanton criminals hung on crosses in excruciating agony on either side of Jesus, who also was suffering the greatest possible pain and dereliction. One of those criminals ordered Jesus to save himself, and them. The other, however, filled with the Holy Spirit, rebuked his fellow criminal, saying, "Have you no fear of God, for you are subject to the same condemnation? Indeed, we have been condemned justly...but this man has done nothing criminal" (Luke 23:40-41). He then pleaded, "Jesus, remember me when you come into your kingdom" (23:42).

What an act of faith! Did he really expect Jesus to welcome him in heaven? No matter, the Lord is always and all-forgiving. "Amen, I say to you, today you will be with me in Paradise" (22:43). Even at the hour of death, Jesus will wipe away every offense if we are truly sorry and repentant. The power of God's forgiveness never ends. There could not be anything more comforting to us than that.

(Note: One criminal has been called Gestas, the other one Dismas, who is recognized as a saint by the Roman Catholic Church,)

A Final Word

In this work, I have discussed that the parables in the three synoptic gospels and the metaphors in John's gospels contain much more than the words themselves. All are rich in deeper meanings and are treasure troves of the words of our Divine Savior. It is my hope you will see the contents of the four gospels in a brighter light and will look beneath the surface every time you read the immortal words of Matthew, Mark, Luke and John.

"Faith" is not just a word; it is a way of life. That is what the gospels stress through the words and actions of Jesus, giving us a firm guideline for living a good and productive spiritual life and being charitable in our generosity for and to others. God is always there to show us the way to eternal happiness. Embrace your spiritual gifts with happiness and joy every day.

May God bless you always and in all ways.

CPSIA information can be obtained
at www.ICGtesting.com
Printed in the USA
FSHW021510210121
77747FS